LIVING ABOVE WORRY

David A. Robertson

John 3:30

David H. Patterson, PhD

LIVING ABOVE WORRY

how ascending faith
can make your life
anxiety-free

TATE PUBLISHING & Enterprises

Table of Contents

Introduction

As a believer in Christ Jesus, should you be asked today, "Do you believe the Bible teaches you are not to steal or you are not to kill or bear false witness?" you would answer with a very strong *yes*. However, should I ask, "Do you believe it is a sin to worry?" many of you would answer *no*. Then you would set out to prove your response. The most common response would be to justify ourselves in our worry with statements like, "After all, everyone else is doing the same," or, "I have always been like this." Worry is so common in our world today that few stop to ask the question, What is the alternative to this miserable habit called worry? No doubt some will become so used to dealing with worry that they would worry if there was nothing to worry about.

If a poll was taken in *USA Today*, most of this nation would admit to worrying on a daily basis. It is true, however, that the same lips that gave us the Ten Commandments said to us in Matthew's gospel, chapter six, "Do not worry." In fact, in ten verses, He repeats it three times and gave three examples to show us just how foolish and needless it is to worry.

Worry has become a very common guest in our homes and in most of our lives. The fallout of this great tragedy is one of the most, if not the most, revealing fault in our lives. In the following pages, I want to share with you what I have learned from God's Word and experiences and from many hours of silence in His presence asking for wisdom on this subject so I could help others understand His heart and gain His directions for learning to live above worry. I will try to help you understand the difference between worry and concern. We can acknowledge there is a difference between concern, which at times can exhibit the stirring of God's Spirit in our hearts, and worry, which is evidence of a lack of trust—such a lack of trust that I believe it is a sin. We would be wise not to ignore God's offer to walk with us and to fellowship with us. This is His way of directing us to trust Him and become aware of His presence. To fail to grow in His grace and knowledge is a sin. To toss and turn night after night on a bed of sorrow after reading His promise to never leave us nor forsake us (Hebrews 13:5) is a sin. It is an insult to our Savior to be so out of touch with His great and wonderful gifts that we live day after day and year after year in the same spiritual defeat as the rest of the unbelieving world.

God allows us to experience pain in order to help us understand that something is physically wrong. With this awareness, we go to a physician for help and correction. We grow tired and weak, which tells us it is time to rest. Our stomachs will make all kinds of noise, usually on Sunday morning between 11:00 a.m. and noon, telling us we need fuel to rebuild our energy and strength. There are times we get so hungry for His closeness that we are driven to some special place or activity that will allow us to renew that warmth and love that is undeniably His special touch on our lives.

Worry is allowed so we can be made aware of the danger of losing His leading in our lives, resulting in some physical as well as spiritual abnormality. It is the warning for us to cease living with doubt and fear. It is a warning for us to come to Him and wait in prayer until the fear is lifted and the tears are gone.

Worry is evidence that we have failed to use the trust our dear Lord Jesus has placed within us. We need to express our trust in the Lord by learning to use our faith in His love for us and His power to meet the needs in our lives.

All that we embrace as Christians involves this subject of trust. Some have suggested that just repeating some words implying our belief in Him will result in salvation. When we spend time in God's Word, we will see how He made the effort to gain man's trust in every generation, not just for salvation, but in all of life's events. He declared Himself to be the Way, the Truth, and the Life in John 14:6. In everything we can and should trust Him completely. Prayer is essential for every believer to grow and be equipped with the tools to live in victory and to enjoy fellowship with our Lord Jesus. Trust is essential to successful praying. No matter the length of our prayers or the intensity with which we pray, if we do not have trust in His ability to hear and answer that prayer, it is a waste of our time. Learning to live in an abiding trust in Jesus will enable us to avoid worry and anxiety. In the eleventh chapter of Hebrews, God gives us a list of characters who used their faith in God to get them through some sticky situations. There was no admixture, just simple trust in God. Study the life of these characters and you will realize they enjoyed a faith greater than simple faith, a faith that is unusual for many today. I have seen the commitment made by each of these people in Hebrews 11, unleashing the power of God in honoring their faith. I have also been made to realize there is a faith greater in its own way than the fundamental faith used in the lives of most of God's children today. I call it an ascending faith that allows us to see the presence of the Lord right here with us, every day, and in every situation. Without this ascending faith, we can never rise into the realm of living above worry and anxiety. Our time spent together will be well spent, and the results offered, if taken and applied, will forever change your life and your service to our wonderful Master.

Living Above Worry

God does not intend for His children to live with worry. Should I ask you today if you believe, "Thou shalt not steal, or kill, or lie, or commit immorality," is the command of God, you would answer *yes*. As well you should. But should I ask, "Do you believe, 'Thou shalt not worry,' is God's command?" many would not accept the thought. However, the same lips that gave us the Mosaic Law give us this command in Matthew, chapter six. In fact, He repeats it three times for emphasis and clarity in verses twenty-five through thirty-four.

After years in the ministry, I found in these verses an understanding as to the weakness I have experienced in so many aspects of my work for Him. I have worked to build a relationship with the Lord Jesus but always seemed to come up short and could never seem to achieve the closeness I had preached to others so many times. I found in these verses the key to that relationship—it is in our trust for Him.

When our children were small, I would sit them on the top of the refrigerator and encourage them to jump into Daddy's arms. After some persuading, they would let go and leap into my arms. What a feeling of excitement for me to realize they trusted Dad. They both shared with me later how they felt after learning Dad could be trusted to catch them and prevent any harm or injury. As this little event grew, they would stand on the refrigerator, and I would sit on the floor, increasing the distance they would fall before I caught them. But still they would jump. Our children grew up in an environment of peace and comfort. They grew to be adults without ever knowing the fear of being left alone, or with only one parent. They never knew hunger from not having food in the house. They knew they were loved in a very special way, and different from the rest of the world around them. In their pre-teen years, both came to know Christ Jesus as the Lord of their life, and know Him as the source of the protection and provision they had enjoyed.

I now can see how this reflects on the subject at hand. God wants us to trust Him without any reservations, to be willing to do whatever He asks without hesitation or deliberation.

When our grandchildren came along, I continued to teach them to leap into my arms. Our little granddaughter was a classic. In fact, she still is. She would without hesitation jump so hard she could have reached my arms some distance from the refrigerator. I remember one evening when her father came to pick her up and she wanted her dad to see how brave she was. Over and over again, she wanted me to place her on top of the refrigerator, and each time, she would leap as hard as she could, sometimes with her eyes closed, maybe backwards, and other times with her arms folded against her body showing that she had no fear at all, just simple but full trust that I would not allow any harm to come to her. After several jumps, her father, concerned about my growing tired, suggested she jump to him instead of me. She refused. He pleaded for some time, assuring her it would be all right and that he too would catch her. But she would not leap to him. I saw in the father's face the look of hurt and could even hear in his voice the tone of disappointment. I quickly got her interested in something else to avoid more hurt for the dad.

One Saturday not long after that, I was in the front lawn at our home, picking up twigs and leaves blown down by a rainstorm we had the day before. The front porch on one side was some six to seven feet high, and the ground sloped away from the house, making the distance from where I was to the porch at least ten feet, maybe twelve. I heard the gentle voice of my granddaughter say, "Paw Paw." Then I heard the scream of my wife: "David!" I turned in time to see Paige in midair; she had already left the porch in flight to my arms. I quickly caught her, but the force of her weight and the distance she had traveled knocked me to the ground. We rolled over and over from the force of the impact. All the while, she was laughing and then said, "Let's do it again." I talked her out of a repeat performance, but the thought came to my mind and then to my heart, *what trust this child has in me.*

Later that day, I was thinking again about the event with Paige, and it came to me: *This is just what the Lord wants from each of us.* Had there been times I failed to trust Him and grieved His heart the same way the girl's dad was hurt when he was not trusted? Weeping, I confessed my sin to my heavenly Father and asked for help in trusting Him with all my heart.

A parallel can be drawn between our lack of trust and the level of worry that we carry daily in our lives. When I get to the examples the Lord gives us in Matthew chapter 6, I will show how much it matters to Him that we trust Him. His words are so clear and so very strong. I don't know of another subject with such emphasis added. It appears to be as strong as His words about our need for salvation, the forgiveness of sins, and other doctrinal issues.

Excessive worry can lead to depression, and depression unchecked can cause all kinds of physical disorders. Many are sick due to worry and anxiety, and millions more will be diagnosed in coming days with shortness of breath, digestive disorders, artery disease, headaches, and chronic pains that seem to avoid all medical detection. God did not intend that this body be subjected to such worry, and in teaching us to have faith in Him, He encourages us to trust Him to the point that all worry subsides and all anxiety is dispelled forever.

I have heard many stories over the years that were told to show how important it is for us to trust Him. One that I can recall so vividly is about a blind man standing on the edge of a very high cleft on a dark night with no way of knowing how great the fall will be and with no one to help in any way, only the voice he believes to be the Lord Jesus saying, "Jump. I will catch you." His blind, helpless life at stake, he has to make the decision to trust the Lord or not. Can you place yourself in that situation and imagine what your response might be? We all do it every day. We come face to face with decisions that place us in the need to trust our Lord Jesus or face the situations alone without His help. Oftentimes we even try to make ourselves heroes by not wanting to trouble Him with our petty concerns. I repeat; He wants us to trust Him in all things and in every way.

Consider what the Master wants to tell you in the verses we are about to dive into. I pray that God will enable you, as a result of your effort, to learn anew how rewarding it is just to trust Him.

> Therefore, I say unto you, be not anxious for your life, what ye shall eat, or what ye shall drink; nor yet for your body, what ye shall put on. Is not the life more than food, and the body than raiment? Behold the fowls of the air; for they sow not, neither do they reap, nor gather into barns, yet your heavenly Father feedeth them. Are ye not much better than they? Which of you by being anxious can add one cubit unto his stature? And why are ye anxious for raiment? Consider the lilies of the field, how they grow;

they toil not, neither do they spin, And yet I say unto you that even Solomon, in all his glory, was not arrayed like one of these. Wherefore, if God so clothe the grass of the field, which today is, and tomorrow is cast into the oven, shall he not much more clothe you , O ye of little faith? Therefore, be not anxious saying, what shall we eat? Or, what shall we drink? Or, with what shall we be clothed? For after all these things do the Gentiles seek. For your heavenly Father knoweth that ye have need of these things. But seek ye first the kingdom of God, and his righteousness, and all these things shall be added unto you. Be therefore not anxious about tomorrow; for tomorrow will be anxious for the things of itself. Sufficient unto the day is its own evil.

Matthew 6:25-34

So many times I have listened to God's people trying to explain to me a miserable sense of failure. They tried so hard and worked in every way they knew how to achieve an awareness of pleasing the Father and experience success in their Christian pursuit. No matter how committed they were to the work, there was a realization that they had missed the mark and fallen short of their goal. It is evident to me that in many of these experiences, if not all of them, these people were *trying* instead of *trusting*.

There is a place for works in our service for the Lord Jesus, and we all need something to do, but works without trust in Him to bless and guide will not result in our growing closer to Him. The price of true discipleship is not displaying our efforts in a public arena nor in gifts given in secret. The price is, "Take up your cross and follow me." It is in following Jesus as our Lord and Master that leads us into areas of service that require explicit trust. We can go our own way, choose what we want to do, where we serve, or even what we give, but it only brings the desired results when He is leading and we are trusting. In this relationship, He will lead us into such service that we cry out, "I can't do this, Lord." He will reply, "Trust me."

It is in trusting that we gain victory after victory and grow stronger in His love because we are learning to trust and learning to move at the pace He sets for us. Victory is not in gaining the praise or appreciation of the people but in the depths of our hearts, knowing that He is pleased because we did follow Him.

Look around you and see how much worry and fear you can see in the lives of people. See the want and hunger in the world and in the church as well. We are moving fast toward the Lord's return, and the one thing that is moving us faster in that direction is the lack of trust that brings so much unrest, doubt, and selfishness. The trust that activates a sinner's faith is the same trust that will allow him/her to grow in the grace and knowledge of his newfound Lord. There is no place in the Christian's life that one can retire from trusting the Lord Jesus. If God did not intend for us to worry, where does the worry come from? How is it that so many can be so overcome with worry that it is often difficult for them to function in a normal environment? It is no secret. It is revealed in God's Word, and we are going to learn what He has said about the joy of living without worry.

It would be so great if God would allow us to see a life without worry before we embark on the pursuit of that life. Imagine with me for just a moment how great it would be to awaken in the morning with a deep settled peace in your heart, knowing God will be taking care of all your needs today. Without any anxiety you face the day feeling confident that our great creator, God, is in charge and you are safe in His care. You find in His purpose greater reasoning than in your own ideas, and you trust Him with whatever the day brings to you.

In our next chapter we will see via way of God's examples why we should trust Him and never worry.

Overview of Scriptures

In Matthew chapter six, our Lord teaches us to trust Him for all the necessities of life, such as food and shelter and clothing. These are items He wants to provide for us. His advice is to replace worry with seeking His kingdom and His righteousness, and He tells us to enjoy life one day at a time without foolishly using today worrying about tomorrow. Use today for His glory and our good.

The word used in these verses for "take no thought" is *merimnate* in the original language of the Bible. Literally translated, it means do not worry or do not be anxious. It carries the thought of never allowing ourselves to be overly concerned. It is used three times in our text and is given as a strong command from our Lord Jesus. It is not a passing option presented to us but rather a firm command and must be considered by all the family of God.

We need to understand the difference between worry and concern. According to the American Heritage College Dictionary, concern is, "To be of interest or important to; Regard for or interest in someone or something." This is acceptable to the Lord, and we all have matters that concern us or cause us to have an interest in them. When the temperature of our child begins to rise to a high number, we become concerned. If the teenage child is two hours past curfew, we begin to be concerned. Of course, God understands these things. It is at these times we need to learn to trust Him completely. I don't know that our faith will overpower our concern, but it will surely give us peace during the time of concern.

When our concern goes too far or demands too much attention, it has turned into worry. The American Heritage College Dictionary gives the following definition of worry: "Worry is persistent, mental uneasiness, to cause to feel anxious, distressed, or troubled." For the child of God, worry will cause us to deny His Word. Worry nullifies His promise to take care of us. Some may think that worry will enhance His promises or work with the Word to bring us hope. This false notion is not what the Scriptures are teaching us. Worry can and will come from every area of life. There is nothing in our lives that Satan will not use to cause us grief and worry if we allow it.

Please consider with me the time that is wasted on worry that would have been better invested in trusting our Lord. We grow in our ability to trust Him by trusting Him. If we use our time worrying about all the issues we should have been trusting to our Lord, we will never become children of great faith. That is what the devil wants for us, and he will do anything he can to keep us from a life of faith. Some may find in their own life that this is the major way Satan has kept them from growing in the grace and knowledge of Christ Jesus. If we could all go back over the years of our lives and list all the special people we believed to be a great influence on our lives, they would all be people of faith. Worry will keep anyone from becoming the person of faith they want to be.

I have often wondered about the amount of time we have spent worrying. If we could add up all the days and hours, we would realize we have spent months or even years of time worrying about all the things that could have gone wrong and things that could have been lost. Looking back, we can see now that the worry was in vain. God was in charge, and we did not suffer the loss we anticipated. The bills were paid, food was provided, physical care was given, the children were not injured, the roof did not leak, etc.

Our Lord is speaking in this passage about our allowing the material things of life to take priority over everything else in life. When we allow the material things of life to take first place in our allotted time or in our affections, we have overruled the lordship of Christ. We have taken the space He has asked for Himself and given it to things. It is in reality saying, "I will find time for Christ Jesus after I have dealt with all the other things in my life." It is when we learn to give Him first place and love Him more than we do those things we have or things we want that we grow in the faith and lay aside the worries.

One of the most common causes for worry today is becoming so wrapped up in the material aspects of life that we forget about God and eternity. Our Lord Jesus has asked for first place in our lives. He desires to be placed ahead of all possessions and all positions we may hold. If we began to place a priority on everything and everyone in our lives, where would Jesus be on your list? He wants to be first. This may prove difficult for some to do. I hope this book will help advance many in the direction of allowing Him to hold first place, not out of our need to know Him in this way, but our love for Him demanding from us that He be first.

I have found that the motive for many is to possess more than someone else. It isn't so much coveting for themselves but just wanting to be seen as the one who owns more or better things than others. They can find a sense of accomplishment by comparing their wealth with that of others with less. The question arises: do we own these things, or do the things own us? Would having more or having bigger or better things make us of more value to Him? Would it cause Him to love us more than He does now? Would being the owner of bigger or better cars or houses make me a better father or husband? Why is it that we are so tempted to spend valuable time on getting or holding on to things and expect the things to make our lives better? The Bible promises that if we allow the Lord Jesus to be first in our lives, He will give us the things we need.

Jesus is concerned about us becoming so engrossed in getting and having that we lose focus on Him and His kingdom. In becoming so self-centered, we allow anxiousness to rob us of peace, our minds so filled with objects of pride that we lose the ability to rest and ability to have a quiet spirit. We can become so disturbed that we experience a change in our attitude or speech. Our whole demeanor is altered, and we take on the appearance like the rest of the world. Sleep is lost, and we feel pushed day after day to accumulate more and more. This is evidence of the carnal nature of man. The only real hope of controlling the flesh is to submit it to the will of God. When we pursue the things of God rather than attempting to satisfy the desire of the flesh, we build a relationship with the Father. It is in this relationship that we learn to trust Him more and more. The more we trust Him, the less we will be distracted by the things of this world, and the less we will worry.

It is the carnal nature of man to lust for things that we do not have. We are surrounded by people who have no respect for the things of God and live all their lives trying to obtain the things they think will make them happy. We are influenced by some of these people and are tempted to fall into the same deception they have accepted. There is also the desire of the flesh to be in style, to live a standard of life that we think we see others living. Much of what we see in advertisements is a play on this weakness in man. The ads all seem to make such good sense and can make obtaining more, bigger, and better things all seem so easy. The first thing you know the credit card is maxed out, you owe more than you earn, and here you are worried out of your mind as to how you will even meet you obligations. Many do this not only once but again and again, until there appears to be no hope and no way out.

One of the great problems with this lifestyle is that the time we need to meditate on God, time we need for reading and studying God's Word, and time for prayer is consumed by our greed. Little by little, our hunger for the things of God dwindles away. We get to the place that little, if any, time is available for God. He has been pushed out and replaced with material objects that now hold our affections. Without God in our minds and hearts, the demand of the carnal nature will cause us to feel less than those in the world who have more than we do or have bigger and better things than we do. Houses, cars, jobs, and bank accounts all seem to become so important that we spend every effort trying to obtain them, and in the pursuit of these things we forget about our relationship with God. We worry about what the world thinks of us with our older used car and the same house we moved into twenty-five years ago. We worry when the neighbors are leaving for a vacation at some plush resort and we know our vacation will be spent in the backyard pruning trees and trying to get the flowers to grow. Our life just doesn't measure up to the neighbor's.

Quickly rethink this scene. If the neighbor enjoys all this world has to offer but dies in their unbelief, not having enjoyed the love and fellowship of God and missing heaven too, would you really want to trade places with them? God wants us focused on Him and His supply to us. We can have all we need and more and enjoy knowing the source is from our heavenly Father. The latter sounds a lot better to me. The object of Satan is to create such a desire in our hearts for the things of this world that we lose all thought of allowing the Lord to hold first place in our hearts. There is just so much time in a day, and if Satan can cause us to be preoccupied with getting more of the world and its goods, he knows we will not have enough time to think about giving Christ first place, not enough time for prayer and study in God's Word, and not enough time for worship or service for Him. I think Satan is too wise to boldly confront one of God's children with a bold demand to choose from his catalog of worldly goods and fleshly pleasures. God would not let us go so easy. However, when Satan can ever so tactfully lead us just a little moment at a time, until he has us committed to more than we would have ever thought possible, then he allows us to see how far we are from a life committed to God. Many at this point become too ashamed to admit to anyone else the trouble they are in or seek help from a spiritual source.

Hold those precious possessions close to your heart. Embrace them as tightly as you can, and love them as you brag and boast about all that you now have. Can they love you back? Can they stop the tears of a broken heart? Can they comfort your soul when you realize how you have failed Him, the one who is love and has shown you such great love? These things held in such high places of honor in our hearts and minds can rob us from the joy of knowing it was His great love that made those things available to us. It was His goodness that brought them into our lives. That place of honor belongs to Him, but now you have turned away from His gifts and replaced Him with a strange love affair.

God does not want us to be so in love with tangible objects that we forget to love Him more. Loving these objects because of the One who gave them to us places the emphasis on our relationship with God. This pleases the Father and will move Him to give even more of His gifts to His children. This will result in our wealth accumulating in heaven rather than on earth. Our blessing will not be hidden from view in some bank but will be reserved in heaven for us, where all the redeemed will have view.

The peace that once brought music to your soul has been replaced with fear and is standing guard to protect what you have worked so hard to gain. Much of life is formed around the things we hold dear. If you should learn someone is attempting to take from you that which you worked so hard to gain, your life will be spent trying to protect your wealth. If your wealth has, on the other hand, been given by God and protected by Him, there is no need for you to be worried about it. All your time can be spent enjoying the gifts of God. If God has given a bigger car or better home to a neighbor than He has given to you, rejoice in knowing the goodness of God. This will only increase your peace and dispel any worry you may have had. Knowing God is good and fair in all His gifts to man, you will have no need to worry about anything your neighbor has nor feel any less important in God's eyes. The way to achieve this is to stay focused on God, not on the neighbor. What the neighbor has or thinks does not reflect on us. God is not going to judge us by what others in the neighborhood have or do. Stay focused on the source of all our blessings, remembering all the while if you have been faithful you have all God intends for you to have at this point in life. If more is needed, God will provide. Allowing Him to see our hearts satisfied with what He has already given will only encourage Him to trust us with more.

There is a story about this in Luke's gospel, chapter twelve. The importance of this passage is to show us that a man who is so focused on getting more and more of this world's goods does not consider his relationship with God. Why would he feel any need for help from anyone so far as worldly goods is concerned? His problem is not in the amount of his wealth but in his relationship with God. He is so blinded by his possessions and the envy of his neighbors that he has forgotten about God.

He would have been better off to have died a poor man in good standing with God than a rich man with no faith in God and no awareness of needing God. The only worry in his life is trying to keep what he has gained and keeping the envy and respect of the neighbors. If all in his community knew of this man's lack of faith and the selfish way he lived, he would not be envied nor respected. His worry is manifested in his soul. He is speaking to his soul, trying to suggest ease and peace because he has no peace. He is so preoccupied with what he has and who he thinks himself to be that he has ignored the truth. He is worried about his barns not being big enough to hold what he has produced. He is seeking peace and pleasure as the result of having so much and is about to learn that God is not impressed with the amounts of whatever we accumulate.

There may be pleasure in sin for a season, but real pleasure comes from God, and there is not lasting peace, save the peace of God that is given to the believer as God's gifts. This man is proof to all of us that possessions cannot satisfy the desire of our soul. He had more than everyone in his community and yet was troubled in his soul. What the world can give us will never produce God's peace in our hearts. Only what God gives will last for eternity. Only those riches we have reserved in heaven will matter in eternity. Life here at its best will not exceed one hundred years. What is that compared to a never-ending eternity? God thought the man in this story was foolish for applying so much of his effort to obtaining as much of this world's goods as he could. He thought it would bring him an easy life and much security but learned he faced a sudden entry into eternity without anything that pleased God.

This worried man in Luke twelve made four terrible mistakes: (1) He preferred his body to his soul. Eating, drinking, attending all the best parties, and making a name for himself on earth were what mattered the most. Examine your heart to see if it is real peace with God that you desire. See if you have placed a price on His love and affection that is greater than your desire for more of this world. I know some will say they want both, but the simple truth is one will have the preeminence and the one which we deem the greatest will get most of our time and affection.

(2) He preferred the world to God. In fact, the world became his god. I don't mean to say that he forgot all about God. He would still attend worship on Easter and Christmas and on both occasions would put something in the offering plate, making sure others could see him in action. His joy and peace now came from the world. There were no communications from heaven.

(3) He preferred time to eternity. He was living as though he would never leave this world. One thing I have seen everywhere I have been is cemeteries. People are dying all over the world. No one stays here forever. You are going somewhere, maybe soon. You can't stay here. Why store up treasures here when we know we will have to leave one day? In so many meetings I have attended, the conversations were so much alike. Where did you go for the weekend, or what show did you see, all about self and self-indulgence. The name of the game today seems to be entertainment and pleasure. No thought of heaven, no interest in investments in God's city. Some of these same people will die with the expectation of receiving God's "Well done my good and faithful servant." Oh, that we could learn to live with the knowledge of being citizens in heaven, where our inheritance is being held in reserve by God.

(4) This man lived as if he would never die. He forgot that he was mortal. He had forgotten about the brevity of life. He had placed material value on all that he had, even his soul. No matter what our thinking may be, no matter how committed we are to our pursuit of pleasures, we must all give an account to God for our time here on earth. This man had gathered treasures

but lost them, his soul, and God. Enriching himself outwardly, he improvised himself inside. Linking himself with perishable things, he perished with them. I read somewhere: A wise man desires no more than he may get justly, use soberly, distribute cheerfully, and leave contentedly.

Unlike many of the world that are worried about getting more of the world's goods and some who are truly worried about getting even the necessities of life, this man was only worried about keeping what he had gained and keeping his status before the eyes of his community. I doubt if anyone could explain the difference between the two kinds of worry. In fact, they are no doubt the same in moral value. With the rich man, his worry is for those who want what he has and how he will be able to hold on to it. With the poorer man, worry will be finding a way to take from the rich man what he has. The carnal man must realize that what he now wants of this world's goods someone else now owns. In reality he is wanting to find a way to get it away from someone else so he can claim it as his own possession. The one who now owns the wealth must figure out a way to keep others from taking his wealth. The man who trusts God and is not consumed with greed and is not worried about the world trying to take his wealth from him is the one living in peace. He is living above worry.

Listen to this man carefully, lest you think he is not worrying. More than most examples given in the Scriptures, this man is tormented by the fact he has invested his life seeking things, believing they would bring him purpose and social status, only to find out too late he was mistaken. His words weep with the sound of mourning and trouble of soul. He was facing eternity without faith, only spiritual failure. God did not think him weak, uneducated, or without skill. God thought him a fool because he was so busy earning his wealth that he forgot about his soul.

The message in this passage is simple: only God can satisfy the craving of a soul.

The question is asked in the Bible, Luke 9:25, "For what is a man profited if he gain the whole world and lose himself, or be a castaway?" And again in Proverbs 10:2, "Treasures of wickedness profit nothing, but righteousness delivers from death." Worry is not always manifested in an outward expression easy for anyone to see. It is often masked, renamed, and hidden in dark recesses of the mind and heart. Worry is not always about things we know we lack when compared to others or even compared to our own desires. Worry can often be manifested by the lack of peace God has promised and the absence of contentment in our hearts. Worry will always be present in the self-indulgent life. To be self-centered is a choice that makes it impossible to be God-centered at the same time. Without God as the mainstay in a life, there will be unseen negatives that will torment the soul of man.

God has said in Matthew 6:33, "But seek you first the kingdom of God and His righteousness, and all these things shall be added unto you." God really cares about you having the necessary things of life, and He will provide these necessities when we trust Him. In some cases, He may also give the items of luxury, as long as they do not lead to extravagance and self-indulgence.

Food, clothing, a place to live, and having our medical needs met are necessities of life. It cannot be wrong in God's eyes for us to work for these items, not only to provide for the need, but also to secure them for our tomorrows. What is wrong is when we neglect God and do not involve Him in the process of obtaining these items. Some can work long hours, put in overtime, and even take on extra work and second jobs, just to keep all that we have and make sure we continue to accumulate at the pace we have grown comfortable with. Instead of thanking God for the blessing we enjoy, we spend more time asking Him to help us get more and better and bigger and ask for His protection on that which we have already put back in store. When we do this, usually we neglect others. We are blind and deaf to the sight and cry of a man in need or a soul suffering. It is as if the only tears we can hear are our own. The only pain we can feel is that within our own bodies.

There is a passage of Scripture in Matthew 6:19–24 that speaks to this thought. It will be good if we consider these verses before we get into the subject of living above worry.

We Are Not To Lay Up Treasures On Earth

Lay not up for yourselves treasures upon earth, where moth and rust does corrupt, and where thieves break through and steal. But lay up for yourselves treasures in heaven, where neither moth nor rust does corrupt, and where thieves do not break through nor steal. For where your treasure is, there will your heart be also. No man can serve two masters; for either he will hate the one, and love the other; or else he will hold to the one, and despise the other. You cannot serve God and money.

Matthew 6:19–24

We are introduced here to two different kinds of treasures, those on earth and those in heaven. I will address those in heaven in just a little while.

There are also two kinds of relationships between man and his treasure. He hates one and loves the other.

There are two kinds of service. He will hold one and despise the other.

These verses require us to consider our priorities. Where have we made the largest investment of time and service? Where have we invested the larger portion of our money? Who is it that gets first place in our hearts? I am not suggesting that we look at these questions with a comparison of dollar for dollar or minute for minute. God knows there are necessities we must obtain and there are other demands on our time, but in all the areas of life, we choose where the Lord is. We decide what part He is to play in the unfolding of our days, months, and years.

Some can go through life committed to their own agenda, which God is completely left out of. They will wait until it is time to die and then become concerned about their relationship with God. I have learned the way to have Jesus in the boat when the storms come is to get Him into the boat while there is calm. He will be there when the storms of life come, and they will come.

Jesus said, "You cannot serve two masters." Don't try to twist that into something that will allow you to go on grabbing all you can of this world while neglecting God. Face the fact that we are all enslaved to one of the two. We love one of the two. We hold to one of the two but not both. It cannot be so. Explain it away if you can, but sooner or later, you will come to face the fact of which one you have loved and served. When it is not of God, that pursuit becomes an idol in our life. We will worship at the altar of money or some treasure, just as real as when we sit in the pew at church to worship God. In fact, I believe there are some at church still worshipping their idols instead of God.

It hurts me to say it, but honest I must be; I fear there are even some in the pulpits of our nation that are worshipping gods of this world instead of the living God of eternity. I have heard it said, "An idol is anything we love, serve, or fear more than we do God." This person has a heart so full of worry and a life so filled with anxiety they must be among the most miserable on earth.

Please think with me on this: any life that is not being lived for God's purpose and is not being lived to bring pleasure to the heart of God is a life of constant worry. In any absence of God's peace, carnal worry and the deceitfulness of riches take over the will and the mind of man. If pleasing God is not the pursuit of man, then pleasing himself will be. There can be no peace in the heart of a man who has forgotten God.

Jeremiah asks the question in his prophecy, chapter two and verse thirty two, "Can a maid forget her ornaments, or a bride her attire? Yet my people have forgotten me, days without number." To forget God means there is no restraint on the will of man. His goal becomes self-indulgence and to gain all that will please the flesh. What may seem to be contentment is the hollow expression of the face, void the truth from his heart. If he should be able to ignore all the truths of God and live void of a conscience, he may be able to tell the world he knows no worry or care. However, when the first thought of eternity comes to his mind, he will experience worry as never thought possible.

Many today seem to think that a life that knows no material need is a life without worry. This is not true. A life filled with the things of earth but void of the life of God within their soul can be the life most filled with worry. It may appear as an unsettled spirit or just an uneasiness, but the fact that something vital is missing in that life will cause worry on a critical level. It is often in these lives that substitutes are sought in an effort to find an ease for the troubled conscience, resulting in various types of addictions.

Our lives will be filled with worry and anxiety until we learn to come fully in the face of God with full trust, destroying all the idols, all the strongholds, and all the influence of evil, until we can yield our all to Him. But when he finds Jesus, he will search no more.

Should a man work for all the things he thinks would bring him pleasure, only to learn he has labored in vain and all he has achieved has not produced one moment of joy or peace, he will try even harder to produce what his soul craves, not knowing it is all in vain. This man is searching, but he does not know what he is searching for. His quest in life will only produce more thirst and greater desire but without any relief until he learns what he is thirsting for. This void in his heart and thirst in his soul will produce an anxiety that can consume the life and soul of man. Of all the many evidences of worry, this one is possibly the most dreaded.

In many of life's problems, there are several methods of finding relief. When a man doesn't know the object of his search, he is as a blind man in a dark room looking for a black cat that isn't there. He will not find anything to satisfy until he finds the saving grace of our Lord Jesus. He cannot find it in a bottle, nor can he find peace in his pills. He may gather around him people who would be his friends but find only disappointment and despair. But when he finds Jesus his search will end, and his hunger will be satisfied.

As to the treasure in heaven, allow me to get some help from Simon Peter. In his first epistle, chapter one and verses three through five, we read:

> Blessed be the God and Father of our Lord Jesus Christ, which according to his abundant mercy hath begotten us again unto a lively hope by the resurrection of Jesus Christ from the dead. To an inheritance incorruptible, and undefiled, and that fadeth not away, reserved in heaven for you. Who are kept by the power of God through faith unto salvation ready to be revealed in the last time.

Peter is writing about the glorious hope of all believers. Please keep in mind as we travel through these rich and rewarding verses that we are working toward a worry-free life. Peter's contribution will help us focus our minds and hearts on something other than this world and what it offers. When we begin to realize all that we have in this inheritance Peter is writing about, we can never again think that we are in need or have reason to worry about anything.

This lively hope, or better said, a living hope, is not the wishful thinking that we are guilty of. It is in reality defined as "God's permission to expect." It works in conjunction with our free moral agency or our right to choose. When God created all that is, He placed in man alone the privilege of choice. Nothing else that God made has the right to choose. There is an instinct placed in the animal world and a bent to respond to design in all of the plant world. They all just respond to the way they are made, never making any choices as man does. There is one supreme reason for this.

God could have made man like all else He had made. That would have made mankind as a puppet with design for man to worship, love, and serve his Creator. In this state of mind, there would have been neither love nor honor for God. If we were forced to serve Him by our created form, how would it be considered service? It would just be conscripted labor. It was and is God's desire that man choose Him as Lord and serve Him as Master and love Him as Redeemer and Friend. He created us with the ability to choose Him or deny Him. The rewards for choosing His great love are so many the libraries of the world could not hold all the splendor and glory He has made for us.

Peter writes about this living hope and describes it as our ever ongoing hope, that which God has in store for us and is being held by Himself, awaiting our entrance into eternity. Now here is the major thought of this passage: It is there in heaven *now*;

it is ours *now*; we own it because He has given it to us *now*. We are not just going to receive this special inheritance; we have it already given and in store, waiting for us to arrive home.

When we stay focused on this world, with all of our losses, our pains, and our problems, anyone would worry. Most of us would experience an emotional collapse. What Peter is saying makes a lot of sense to me, especially when dealing with the subject of worry. If we focus on what the Lord has done and what our inheritance in Him is, how could we ever stay down or allow ourselves to become discouraged?

We are "heirs of God, and join heirs with Christ Jesus" (Romans 8:17). It is so easy to get caught up in the affairs of this world and forget that we are also citizens of heaven. What a privilege to know that we shall live forever and live with Him and with all the provisions He has prepared for us. We can truly believe that just His presence would make it a glorious heaven, but when we dig into the Word and see all that He has done for us, we will begin to live like the King's children rather than defeated and discouraged people. The same hope we have there we have now. The same promise we have there we have now. The same provisions we have there we have now. The same Spirit of the Living God we have there we have now. The Lord that we yield to there we should be yielding to now. This is an ever active life that really exists. It lives now in the heart of every believer and will live there forever in heaven. It is *eternal life*, God's life.

Peter tells us that it is God's mercy that has "begotten us again" unto this hope. Do not be misled on this thought. Peter is talking about being born again. "Begotten again" is born again. We were born once into this fleshly body; we must be born again into the spiritual life of God. This is eternal life.

When Jesus was raised from the dead, He set a standard for all of His children to follow. Because He was raised, we too shall be raised from death to life. Because Christ was raised by the power of God the Father, we too shall be raised by the power of God the Father. How could we ever worry about death when we know that we shall not be left in death? Death is dead to a believer. Death died when Jesus arose from the dead. Our inheritance is not one of death but an inheritance of life, eternal life.

I had been called to a patient's room in the hospital to comfort a dying lady. After some words with her and a time of prayer, I walked out of the room with the patient's physician, a man from another culture and another faith. He placed his hand on my shoulder just outside the room and asked, "If you Christians really believe what you say you believe about heaven, why are you so reluctant to die?" I did give some insight and explanation to the doctor, but in my heart, I was saying, *He is right*. If we could learn to focus on the life we have in Him instead of the life we are forging for ourselves here in this world, we could be free from the fear of death.

I have seen people allow themselves to experience untold pain and prolonged treatment just to add a few days, maybe just a few hours to this life. Not all of God's children will do this. I have known some who will not stay one minute more than demanded in this world. It is because they are fully aware of their citizenship in heaven. They have taken biblical inventory of the inheritance awaiting them, and they are eager to go home.

I can remember as a very young man talking with my grandmother, who was near death. She said the day would come, as it had with her, that I would have more friends and family in heaven than I did on earth. That would make it easier for me to go home. That has already happened in my life, and I know that many can identify with that thought. When I add into the picture the fact of seeing our wonderful Lord Jesus and living in His presence forever, there just isn't much to make me want to stay here one day longer than needed.

We believers have submitted our lives to the One sitting at the right hand of God in the throne room of heaven. God is not just in heaven. He is everywhere, all around us, wanting to take care of us, wanting to relate to us in every area of life. We hear a lot today about spiritual gifts, but what about this greatest gift of all, the gift of eternal life? Our experiences here are just the beginning, and there is no end. The life and hope we have in Christ is not changing from God's point of view when we die. We just move into the kind of life that will allow Him to bestow on us the fullness of His purpose and plan. Eternal life does not begin in heaven; it begins here in this world. Eternal life has many benefits for this world but also for the world to come. There should be no more worry in our life now than what we will know in the life to come. No doubt it will be impossible for anyone to worry in heaven, and if we were able to focus clearly on Him and His purpose in our life, we could lose the worry we have added into our lives now due to the lack of trust.

A physician asked me how I knew God would take my soul into heaven and one day raise my body from the dead. I answered, "Because He showed me His plan when He raised Jesus from the dead." He clears the way for all of us who will follow after Him. After Jesus was raised from the dead, He ascended into heaven and is seated by the Father's right hand. He is ever interceding for each of His followers. We are seen in the Beloved. That is to say, God sees us as part of, or partakers of, the life, death, and resurrection of Jesus Christ. As His followers and receivers of His glorious gift of eternal life, we will share with Him for all eternity all the joys and all the glory that God has bestowed on the Son, being heirs of God and joint heirs with Christ Jesus.

We have an inheritance now in heaven being held for us by God Himself. Peter describes it as "incorruptible, and undefiled, and that fades not away, reserved in heaven for you." Incorruptible (*aphtharton*) means it cannot become corrupted or die. It cannot ever cease to exist. Keep in mind it is there now, waiting for every child of God to enjoy. We can bank on it.

I have met so many people that I believe have more money than I do on this earth. Of course, it would not require them to have a great deal of money to make that statement true. However, I have never met a person who has more of an inheritance than I do. Nor do I believe that I have any more than another believer in Christ Jesus. The glorious thought is it is there now, it is ours now, and it will be there when we get home. No one can mess with it or change it in any way. It is being held by God Himself.

Can you think of anyone bigger than God? Is there any force known to man that could overpower God and do damage to our inheritance? Rejoice, rejoice, my friend; what God has done for us is ours forever and will not fade away. It is recession-proof and is not harmed by any political movement. It is beyond being tampered with. Peter says it is undefiled (*amianton*), meaning it cannot be polluted or ever lose its value or purpose.

It is normal for the world to worry about keeping their worldly goods, worry about a thief taking what they claim as their own wealth, or perhaps worry about their stocks, bonds, and savings accounts at the bank. However, the child of God who has invested in eternity and lives with the peace of knowing those investments will last forever and cannot be disturbed. All the grace, mercy, and peace God has invested in our lives are held in reserve for us, and there is no possible need to worry about anyone taking it from us. When we become fully aware of this fact, we will find it very difficult to worry about anything.

What God has given us cannot be taken from us. To do so would imply something or someone is greater than God. This is simply not true. If He is the keeper of all that is dear to us, who or what is stronger that it might take from us what God has given and now protects? Why worry as the world does? We are different from the world. A defeated life is not evidence of faith in God; it is evidence of a failing trust or the absence of trust. God cannot fail! We are the product of His faith, and living in that faith cannot produce failure or loss. As humans we may view the things of life wrongly, but in the reality of eternity, we are not losers, nor can we be. "We are more than conquerors through Him that loves us" (Romans 8:37).

Our home was broken into while the wife and I were at work. The thieves took most of my wife's jewelry and some loose coins we had. The loss was considerable for us, more sentimental than actual value, but the feeling of someone invading our home and taking what was not theirs to take left a tremendous feeling of defilement. The very next day, we began to clean in every area of the house where the thieves had been. It was, to us, contaminated and dirty. This can never happen to our eternal inheritance. It is under the watchful eyes of God Himself, and it cannot be tampered with. There is no need to worry about that which God has purposed for us.

Now if God knows all and He knows all before it comes to pass, then He knows what we are facing or what we are going through. If we trust Him, there is no worry because He has our best interest at heart and will not allow anything to happen to us that would take Him by surprise. We can trust God about today and tomorrow because He did not fail us yesterday.

When God was talking with Moses in Exodus 3:15, He said to Moses, "Thus shall you say unto the children of Israel, The Lord God of your fathers, the God of Abraham, the God of Isaac, and the God of Jacob, has sent me unto you, this is my name forever, and this is my memorial unto all generations." God is saying, "I am the God of continuity." In other places, He proclaims that He is the "Lord thy God, I change not." The only reason a sound mind would ever want to change something is if change could make it better or worth more. God is perfect and will not change because He needs no changes.

Throughout the Scriptures, God give us His assurance that He will not fail and He will not forsake us. Being kept by His power tells us that we will not fail or come short of His expectations. God's power keeps us, and it is His power that keeps our inheritance. In all of life's temptations, trials, and disappointments, we are being kept by His power. It is His sovereign promise and power that He will keep our inheritance and keep it so that we do not suffer loss. There can be no doubt in any of our minds or our hearts that God is able do exceedingly above all that we could think or ask.

The problem arises when it comes down to believing that He will indeed do what we have asked. Christ says, "Ask and you shall receive." James says, "You ask and receive not because you ask amiss, that you may consume it upon your lust" (James 5:3). Our focus is usually on that which we do not have, or we focus on what someone else has and we think it to be bigger, better, or of greater value than what we have and want the same or better for ourselves. The point Christ wants to make with us is consider what you have, what we have now as His children, reserved in heaven for us. When we can walk down the street fully aware of our inheritance, fully trusting our great God to give what we need for the day and leaving tomorrow's needs to tomorrow, we can wear a smile of success that transcends everything in this world.

Maybe here is the time to admit a few things to ourselves: would you rather drive an expensive car and wear the latest fashions and have your pockets full of money than enjoy the knowledge of your inheritance in heaven? Is having it now more important than the truth of what He has laid up for us? Those things purchased on the cross and purchased in His sinless life and paid for with His own blood are, or should be, of far greater value to the children of God than the wealth of a million worlds.

One of the difficulties we will deal with on the subject of worry is the problem of so many of us in the family of God who are living like orphans. We allow the world to look at us with contempt, and we look at the world with envy, as if we had nothing of our own. I was raised in east Tennessee, one of eight children in our family. New clothes were a luxury, and I don't ever remember being concerned about what was fashionable. I do remember having clean clothes to wear every day. I thought patches were something to be proud of, especially when I knew what garment was cut up to make the patches. The teachers at school and the people in our church would often make mention of the fact that all the children in our family were always clean. Mom and Dad did the best they could to provide for us, and often at the expense of doing without things for themselves. I was taught even then as a small child about the great things God has in store for His family, and I was part of His family. Somehow, even in those early years, I began to realize how special it is to belong to the Lord Jesus.

The real life is the spiritual life God has in store for us. We get a taste of it here and now, but we are fully invested in the life to come when we leave this world. When we begin our new life in heaven, all the carnal habits of this world will cease. There in that new life, we will never know envy or desire for carnal things. There will be no competition to see who has the best or the most of anything. We will never envy what others have and never make comparison to see if we have more or less than someone else. Heaven's peace is what we can have a little of here and now if we can learn to live above worry. We can have small pieces of heaven's peace in this life, inserted between all the struggles to stay on our schedule. Most believers can relate to the fleeting moments when the entire world seems at peace and the conflicts are still. In heaven we shall live in the continuous, never-ending absence of worry.

God wants us to see His gifts already given, both in this world and the world to come, and stop worrying. Live with the strong assurance that we are victorious in Him; now, today, we are victorious, and our life is full of His great gifts and the inheritance He has laid up for us. Again, I ask that we focus on these facts given to us in His Word, facts that cannot fail or ever be taken from us. While we focus on these truths, set your priorities. Do not allow the flesh to set your priorities. Do not allow the carnal nature of greed or envy to set your priorities. Do not allow the feelings from the past or feelings of having less than others around you to set your priorities. Get out of the negative mindset and think of the promises of God, and then begin making a new set of priorities.

Learn to walk down the streets of any city with the awareness of being royalty, the child of the great King of kings and Lord of lords. We are heirs of God and joint heirs with Christ Jesus. Life here is so brief compared to eternity; why make so much out of this short span of years? We live, work, and invest in this world and this life as if we will live here forever. We stuff into the banks or stock markets all we can get our hands on, believing, or at least hoping, that we can strike it rich and live a life of ease. That ease comes when we have lived according to His standard and principles, when we have invested in eternity and know that we cannot lose on those investments. His peace is given on the principles of His promise, not our performance. We do not need to wait for heaven to know His riches or His peace. We are fully invested with His promises and His gifts now.

He is so much more able to meet our needs than we could ever be. Even if we had all the monies of the world, it would still be better for Him to be our source rather than ourselves. When we begin to live thus, we will watch the worry dissipate and fade away.

When we choose the direction of our service, whether it be the pursuit of riches or obedience to God, we have also chosen our Master. The Bible teaches with strong language, "You cannot serve God and mammon." The choice we make reveals our true Master. If we choose the abundance of this world and that which we store up for carnal pleasures, we have declared that God is not our Master. This is a revelation of our true character. That which we are in the heart will surface at the moment we make the choice.

There are so many that seem to have the idea of being an exception to the rule of God. They want to believe they can pursue the world, working day and night, consumed in the obtaining more and more of the world, but as long as they give a little of it to the Lord's work and if they attend church on occasion, they have become the exception to the rule. Not so! God has said you cannot serve Him and the riches of the world at the same time. Neither is this a 5-1-1 arrangement—five days for the world (mammon), one day for the family, and one day for God. You may think you are one of those exceptions that give God all the praise for their successes but are nonetheless committed to the carnal drive for more and more riches. With this drive comes all the worries of considering what may happen if you fail. What may happen if the stock market fails and you suffer great loss?

The more you worry, the harder you work, and the less God plays a part in your life. When we choose to serve God, it is with our heart. God wants to live and dwell in our hearts. His peace begins to stir in our lives by renewing our heart. When we find His peace in our hearts, it begins to move into our mind, and then our expressions of life are changed, so much so that all those around us see the difference. The closer someone is to us, the more they can see the change in us because of His peace. This is all due to the fact that we are completely attached to the right master.

Men who love this world and its goods will express a displeasure toward the things of God in a careful way, choosing their words so as not to be offensive, but offensive they are to God.

Having no sense of need for God in their life, they become critical of those of us who admit our need for God. It becomes needful in their mind to express their success without God and put down all who admit a dependence on God. Their loyalty to their own Godless system requires them to speak negatively of those who openly follow the Lord God. When you love the one master, you will hate the other. Your service cannot be divided. God will have all of you or none at all. It appears to be the norm for today. People who name the Name of Christ as their Lord but refuse to separate unto Him want to embrace the public idea of Christianity but hold on to the habits and lifestyle of the world. The Scriptures call us to leave the systems of the world and live a life pleasing to our Lord Jesus Christ. His peace comes into our hearts and minds when we are living the life of faith.

Now here is a sticky thought, and I fear it may affect more than we may have imagined, the thought of admixture, trying to blend just enough of the world with your need for God, resulting in having and enjoying a little of each. The truth is, this results in having neither. God desires all of our heart. He is the great Creator, as well as the Redeemer. He has given Himself so completely that He might have claim to all of our heart, mind, and body. He has promised that this complete surrender to Him will bring peace and happiness in this life and in the life to come. With this commitment of service, we express our true attitude. When we yield ourselves to Him totally, it is our testimony of submission and the acknowledgment of His power and position in our hearts.

Can God give a man riches? Yes. There are several men in the Bible that were considered very wealthy. Abraham was said to be the wealthiest man in the Bible. Then, man's wealth was determined by the number of cattle and/or sheep he had, and Abraham possessed a very large herd of livestock. Solomon was another who possessed great wealth. Noted for his great wisdom, he is not often mentioned for his wealth. When God asked him for the desire of his heart, he asked God for wisdom. Because he did not ask for wealth first, God gave him great wealth as well as wisdom. I have known a few in this life that were truly wealthy men and at the same time completely obedient to God. The difference is in the fact that God knows what the man will do with the wealth before He gives it. I have known of at least one man that had great wealth and came to the saving faith in Christ Jesus and changed his manner of life and used much of his acquired wealth to finance the kingdom work of God.

Be very careful when you begin to think that you are one of those rare exceptions. When we have the right priorities and are focused on His plan for our lives, we are wealthy. Real riches cannot be deposited in the bank, nor can they be bought or sold. The riches of mammon appeal to the nature of man and are presented as being present now. However, those riches are of no value whatsoever in service to God. When we compare what the Lord is offering us with that which the world is offering and it begins to look like the world has an advantage, the nature of our hearts is revealed. When our heart is filled with praise and love for the Master, that is what flows from our heart and lips. To realize how gracious He is and has been in our life will cause us to be gracious to those around us. Solomon said, "As a man thinks in his heart, so is he" (Proverbs 23:7).

Only the Holy Spirit living within us could reveal the truth about the programs being offered by both masters. Mammon promises that he can keep you happy with what he alone can give, and he can give in now. No waiting, no delays, and no faith required. His package would appear to be flawless, with all the excitement of being seen by all who know you as successful and happy beyond your dreams. He does not tell you about all the disappointment of loss, theft, and natural deterioration. He does not bring into the equation the fear of someone taking what belongs to you or loss by other means that will leave you in distress, having sleepless nights trying to figure out what to do next to keep from losing more of your wealth. There is the problem of protecting your newfound riches and the pressure of continuing to make all the right investments so your status doesn't slip downward. Public image is now important for your name's sake. It is a reputation you have acquired for being successful, and now you must protect that good name. More and more time is demanded, with less and less time for family, friends, and nothing left for God. No wonder God said, "You cannot serve God and mammon."

We learn to focus on the wealth and the source of that wealth, even when we see there is no way of finding happiness in the love we have acquired for the things of this world. We should focus on building our relationship with God and spend less time trying to acquire the wealth of the world. Life is time and time is precious, too precious to spend most of our time (life) on trying to get more of this world's goods.

Mammon would tempt us with earthly kingdoms and empires with our name inscribed all over as the mighty one who made it all happen. What we have now and what we have accomplished in the past is never enough. We will always want more because the things we are pursuing cannot satisfy the desire of man's heart. This heart is God-shaped and can only be filled by His love and His presence within us.

With each successful investment, we begin immediately to plan for the next quest. At the same time, men of lower lifestyles are trying to find a way to get what the wealthy man has. His hope is to become like the wealthier person, thinking that lifestyle is filled with pleasure. All the while, you must keep up the appearance of being happy and full of life, hiding the worry, the lack of peace, the emptiness of purpose, and the insecurity about your soul and eternity.

The friends you gain during the time you are enjoying the wealth are fickle and will not last. They are there to inflate your ego and try to get a piece of the action. You can rest assured they will eat all the meals you want to buy, enjoy all the toys you care to provide for them, and treat you as the best friend they have ever had until the money runs out or until you wise up and realize that a friend that is bought is not a real friend at all.

When you have riches, people will suddenly appear with advice and suggestions that would lead you to believe the number one desire of their heart is to be your best help ever. Old, rich men can enjoy the pleasure of young, beautiful women and sometimes even be made to believe they are truly loved. But when the money runs out, they will suddenly look so old and unneeded. Wealthy, old women that have lost all but what money can buy in the way of plastic surgery, dye, and special fixes for almost every part of the human body can be the desire of so many younger men friends. But when the riches are gone, so are the young men, along with all the friends they thought they had. However, there is one Friend that will never leave you nor forsake you.

Can you see how this plays into the cause of worry for many today? If life is a pretense and there are no real standards in life, there is reason for worry. Removing that which is not real and that which will not last nor stand with you in the hour of trouble will move you in the direction of living above worry. What a Friend we have in Jesus. There is only one who will not forsake you, only one who does not care if you are poor in this world's goods.

Had God required that I have social prestige before I could be born into His kingdom, I would have not been accepted the night I came to Him needing to be forgiven and cleansed. Had He required of me some measure of skill or talent, I surely would have been passed by and not accepted. If there was a special on salvation that only cost ten cents that special night, I would have had to wait for another time to present myself before the Lord. The truth is, He only required me to trust Him, and He accepted me on the promise of a never-ending trust, not a performance, display, or long list of all the things I had done that were wrong. There has never been a moment that life was so clear and as simple as it was that night. I wish that all could live in the bliss of God's love and forgiveness. It is the one moment of being perfectly clean and without sin. It is the beginning of knowing His power and love and the beginning of learning His purpose for our lives. We can teach our children about this trust in God and help them avoid doubt. It would be like heaven on earth if everyone knew the Lord Jesus as their Savior and Lord and lived all of life in His peace and love. Of course the world will never be like that until Jesus returns to earth and sets up His kingdom on earth, but we can move closer and closer to the life that is worry-free.

Why Worry About Food and Shelter?

"Behold the fowls of the air, for they sow not, neither do they reap, nor gather into barns, yet your heavenly Father feeds them. Are you not much better than they" (Matthew 6:26). We should be ashamed if we allow a bird to get a living from God's hand and we cannot. This example of God's provision is one of the greatest thoughts on the subject in all the Scriptures, if not all the world. "Behold" is in the imperative mood, suggesting to us that this is not a simple request but is, in fact, a command of God. Research the thought, dig into the subject, and learn all you can about the birds. On first sight, it may appear a bit too simple, but on closer consideration, we find a world of truth that we all need to understand and put to practice in our lives.

I believe this example is the strongest and perhaps the most important one. If this lesson is learned, the following two examples will be even easier to accept and put to work in our lives.

Take a look at Psalm 50:11: "I know (*yada*) all the fowls of the mountains; and the wild beasts of the field are mine." This word in the Hebrew language reveals the unlimited knowledge God has on this subject. I believe this is true concerning all subjects, but for now, let us stick with the birds. God was saying in this verse, "I know the birds of the mountains. I know their father, their grandfather, their great-grandfather. I know all the descendants of each bird all the way back to the days of creation when I made the first bird." Now that is a lot of birds and a lot of knowledge. If this was all in print and in front of us today, I am not sure we could understand all the facts involved in this resource of truth. However, we can get the idea of how enormous this thought really is.

When we draw the conclusion He wants us to all reach, we can begin to see why He does not want us to worry. We cannot attain unto the level of God's knowledge; however, should we know the number of birds that have lived from creation unto this day, we could begin to see the value of God's statement that He feeds the birds, and if He cares so much as to feed the birds, how much more does He care for us? Here is some of what I have found. According to Terres, *The Audubon Encyclopedia of North American Birds*, "It is difficult if not impossible to get an accurate count of the total population of a wide spread species..." Given that ornithologists are not even sure how many species there really are in the world—some suggest there are more than ten thousand species—it would be most difficult to estimate total populations. Nevertheless, the same source says that in 1951, "Fisher, a British ornithologist, estimated there are more than 100 billion individual wild birds in the world." And Leonard Wing (1956) estimated that there were about 5.6 billion birds in the United States. Now try to reason as to how much food is required to feed each one of these birds each day and add all the days back to the beginning of time. Of course this is knowledge known only to God, but He has asked us to consider the birds, so it should make us want to understand all we can on the subject. God has said, "His ways are not our ways, neither His thoughts our thoughts" (Isaiah 55:7). This is an enormous comparison between God's love for the birds and His love for man. To search out for proof that God's love will lead a lost man to salvation. For God's children to search out how much He loves us will draw each of us closer to Him and result in strengthening our faith.

There are others verses of Scripture that suggest God has a daily duty to provide for each one of these birds. Some may want to disagree, saying that all God did was to create a natural response in the birds and they all fed on instinct. The truth of the Bible says it differently. Not one bird is lost or misplaced, falls, or dies without God knowing and seeing that individual bird. What a God! This same God who admits to caring so much for the birds He made and cares so much more for you and me gives us reason to lay aside all worry. Why should any of us worry about something God has promised to do for us? If God has promised to care so much for His children, why would we waste time worrying about that which He is taking care of? Why live our lives in despair and heaviness of heart when these things are already taken care of?

Now here is the main thought from our verse in Matthew 6:26: "…your heavenly Father feeds them." When I was a very young boy, my mother gave me a job to do at home. She would lay aside in a special place all the bread that had grown stale. It was my job to crumble the bread into small pieces and distribute it in the back part of the lawn in such a way that many birds could feed on it. There were eight children in our family, and when Mom made bread for a meal, or for several days, depending on what kind of bread she would make, there was a fair quantity of bread. I thought several times that Mom had made extra bread just so there would be some remaining after the meal for the birds. I have often thought back on those years with great pride in Mom's love for the birds. In the truthful application of the passage, I can now see it was not Mom that was feeding the birds, nor was it me feeding the birds at Mom's direction. It was God, moving on the heart of my mother to feel concern for the birds and the need to provide food for them.

I have often been sent to the store to buy fifty-pound bags of seed for my wife to use to feed the birds. There have always been birdfeeders and birdhouses around every home we have lived in. It would seem to me at times that every week or two, we would come home from the store with another birdfeeder or another birdhouse. It appeared to me that my wife had developed a great interest in the birds native to our area. Bluebirds and hummingbirds were her favorites. I thought it was good for her to have a hobby, and it did bring a great pleasure to her, so I was pleased to assist. I was proud of her for having such a desire to help the little birds have food and shelter. Again, the simple truth taught in the passage before us is: God feeds the birds. He may use you or me or anyone else to actually place the food before them, but it is and always will be Him that feeds the birds.

When we talk about larger birds, like the hawk or an eagle, and still other large birds that feed on live animals, it is a quite different approach to feeding the birds. It would be almost impossible for man to provide the kind of food they would need. However, it is not difficult for God to feed these special birds of prey. I have watched it oftentimes on the farm as a hawk would seem to fall out of the sky and catch a mouse or a rabbit in its talon and rise on the speed and strength of his wings to some lofty place, where he would tear the prey and feed on it, all a part of God's plan for feeding the birds. Now consider this: why do you think God would create a bird with an appetite for mice and not make the mouse? Doesn't make sense, does it? Why would God make birds to hunger for seed and not provide the seed for them? Same question, same God; why would God make man with the need for food and drink and not provide for him all that he needs? The application is simple—God will provide food and shelter for all that He has made. If you would see this truth, behold the fowls of the air. They do not sow; that is, they do not plant seed to grow more seed. They do not gather into barns large amount of seed in store for other days to come. They trust their Creator God to provide each day, one day at a time, all they will need to live.

When God was leading the children of Israel out of Egyptian bondage, about the time they reached the land of Elim, between Elim and Sinai, the people began to complain about their hunger. Thinking back on their bondage, they remembered being fed as slaves. Even though the food was not very special, it was given to them by their masters, the Egyptians. When God heard their complaining, He told Moses He would rain bread from heaven for him and the children of Israel. His instructions to Moses and Israel were to go out every day and gather enough bread (manna) for one day only.

The idea here was to teach Israel to trust the Lord God. If they could store up extra bread, there would be some so industrious they would hire others and bring in enough manna for themselves for many months and extra to sell to their neighbors. Before long, there would be a bread factory opened each mile or two along the way to the Promised Land. Man would then be required to work for money, pay for their bread, and pay taxes on everything. Sound familiar to anyone? From the very start, God intended for man to labor, but He also intended for man to trust Him to provide his food and shelter.

When extra manna was gathered, it would spoil before the next day. This again was to show Israel, and us, that God wants our trust fully each and every day.

Later, God provided meat to go with the bread, and to show how gracious He is, He revealed Himself in a cloud by day and a fire by night. God was saying to Israel, "I will give you food to eat and water to drink, I will protect you from all harm, and reveal My presence with you by day and by night; what more would you have Me do?" If you remember the story, you will recall that Israel also needed fresh water all along the way and still found reason to complain.

If we draw a contrast between the carnal nature of man and the provision of God, you will see how different the two are. It is as true today as it was then in the life of Israel. In fact, you can see how far we have drifted from God's intended plan for man by realizing the fact that much of the concept of fully trusting God for provision is a thing of the past. There is no way for us to talk about numbers because it is impossible for anyone to know, but a simple look at the systems of the world will tell you how far we have missed His fullness in blessing us.

If we could add up all the tons of food and gallons of water they would use for the forty years of travel, it would be just as astounding as the amount of food required to feed the birds, as God has promised to do. I am not suggesting that God intended that we should continue to eat manna and quail each day. That was for the journey of a select people for a select period. However, please note that God did just as He promised to do. He is still available to fulfill any and all promises He has made to each of us as His children, so much so that He can say to us in Matthew's gospel, "Do not worry." The only power great enough to keep us from worrying is the power of fully trusting in Him.

The Lord asks the question in verse twenty-six of Matthew chapter six, "Are you not much better than they?" This is an interesting question, for you see He has drawn a comparison between you and all the birds of the world for all times. His question is a rhetorical one, but we need to respond. Each time we read this passage, we should give Him a response: "Yes, Lord. I know I am worth more to You than all the birds." His words should remind us each time we read this passage that He loves us so much more than He does the birds. Allow His words to remind us that He wants to provide food and shelter for us, just as He has provided for the birds. I can hear the Lord saying, "Not one of these birds has died of starvation." His provision is perfect, without the possibility of failing. He has and is demonstrating this by the way He provides for the birds.

He now places the example before us and says, "Behold the fowls of the air. They sow not, neither do they gather into barns…" That is to say, the birds played no part in being fed each day. All they did is show up and eat. The example is so strong in all of its emphasis because the bird does not have the power of reasoning. There is no ability given to the bird for making decisions. The bird instinctively eats each day as God has provided. There is no doubt, no hesitation, no second guessing, and certainly no worrying on the part of the bird, just eating and being sheltered. I guess we could say that eating for the bird is as natural as flying.

This should cause us to realize the strength of God's promise to us. "Do not worry" is God's command to His children, for it is His daily reminder of His love for us. Calvary is wonderful in that God made provision for paying our sin debt and providing access to Himself and to heaven, but here in this passage is His continued, day-to-day promise of caring for us and providing for us the food and shelter we need. If we could walk down the streets of any city and see hundreds of thousands of birds lying around dead and after examination we could conclude they had all died from starvation, we might then have reason to doubt God's words of promise. Go back now to the numbers when we were trying to determine how many billions of tons would be needed to feed the birds and all the water they have needed since the world began. Imagine it all in one place at one time and seeing the enormous accumulation of supply; now add to the pile the dead bodies of all the birds that have lived since the beginning of time, and then, only then, conclude, "I need to worry." God wants us to see that His love for us is greater than His love for the birds. If we added up the number of all the birds that have lived and died since the beginning of time and know their value to God, we could see by way of example how much He loves each of us and how valuable we are to God. No, my friend, there is no way we can justify all the worry and anxiety we have experienced.

Allow me to suggest another numerical example to you. If we could go back to the beginning of time and pull from heaven's records all the minutes, hours, days, months, and years of worry from all the people that have ever lived and place them on one record sheet, what a tremendous number that would be. And every bit of that number would be an insult to Almighty God. His provision for us has been to the extent that we can and should live above worry, and yet He finds us, day after day, worrying over every little thing, even our daily bread and shelter.

I need to add another thought to the example the Lord has made for us about the birds. He says, "They sow not, neither do they reap, nor gather into barns…" They don't, but we do. The Lord shows us it is all right to labor for these provisions. However, our trust is not in the labor alone; we still need His input to have a sufficient amount to eat.

Think for a moment about the power of the seed that God has given us. I must take you to Genesis 1:11: "And God said, Let the earth bring forth vegetation, the herb yielding seed, and the fruit tree yielding fruit after its kind, whose seed is in itself, upon the earth; and it was so." During the time of creation, God created every type of food grown from the soil. The power of His plan was in the seed. My wife has a window ornament shaped like an apple with these words on it: "Man can count the seeds in one apple; God can count the apples in one seed." Creation, in all of its glory and wonder, was not for God's benefit as much as it was for man. Man was His highest form of creation, and man was for Him, not for the earth. God desired to be loved, trusted, and obeyed, so He made man in His own image.

I believe God gave man the power of reasoning. When we see how far man has advanced in technology and science, with all the inventions we have enjoyed in such a short period of time, it appears to me that we must have a little of God's skills built into us, just like the seed has life built into it.

Perhaps the most convincing thought for me comes from Isaiah 1:18: "Come now, and let us reason together, saith the Lord…" The verse is talking about salvation, about having our sins forgiven, and the stain and guilt removed, but notice the invitation is from God to man. The process we are invited to participate in is to reason with God. Can you imagine the power of the mind that has the ability to reason with God? All that God made, He made good, but all that He made, other than man, did not have the power of reasoning and the right to choose. In this verse, He extends an invitation to man to reason with Him on the need to be cleansed from sin. It makes such clear sense to me that the mind of man should possess the ability to make good decisions, especially when it comes to choosing eternal life and freedom from sin. God is ever appealing to the reasoning ability of man to come to Him, and we need to learn to trust Him for all we need.

I must add the fourteenth verse to this passage in Isaiah. It reads, "If you be willing and obedient, you shall eat the good of the land." Here we are again faced with God's promise of provision. Notice also God sets forth the conditions for receiving His provision. It is willingness and obedience. This sets apart the children of God from the rest of the world, as pertaining to provisions. It suggests to me the invitation to live above worry by trusting His plan and accepting His provision and shelter for us, just as He provides for the birds. The only difference is we, as man, must make the choice to trust Him. In doing so, we fulfill the purpose of God in creating man in His own image. When we love Him by choice and serve Him by choice, we have brought great joy to the heart of God.

I believe all that God made serves Him by created design. "The earth is the Lord's, and the fullness there of" (Psalm 24:1). Man, however, must make the choice to serve Him in obedience. It is in this same framework of choosing that we make the choice to trust Him for all we need. It requires the choice. God will not force His provisions on us no more than He will force His salvation on us. You can worry if you want to. Pay all the price of living without His favor and provision, and wonder each day where your supply will come from. But I am so happy to tell you again and again that you don't have to worry. We can rise above it and live in the fullness of His love for us.

When I think of faith in God, I always think of Hebrews chapter eleven. This is the part of Scripture that showcases some of God's people who were found pleasing in God's sight because of their faith. The first verse in Hebrews chapter eleven gives us the meaning of faith: "Now faith is the substance of things hoped for, the evidence of things not seen" (Hebrews 11:1). This is very important because it is the only verse in the Bible that defines for us what faith is. Most of the Bible, when it is referring to men, is either drawing attention to their faith or their lack of faith. Nowhere else in Scripture does God define faith. He says it is the "substance" (*hupostasis*), the foundation or assurance of, or the guarantee of things hoped for. It is the "evidence" (*elegchos*), which means conviction. Therefore, we can see the definition of faith as the assurance of things hoped for and the conviction of things not seen. This is when the mind and heart agree that God will provide what we are in need of. It becomes more real than sight, sound, or feelings.

Be careful here; you cannot make faith happen. Standing and declaring a thing will not make it so. How sad when God's professing people name it and claim it and it doesn't happen. That is neither substance nor conviction, and it is not real. God has given to every one of His children a "measure of faith." He has laid a foundation before us as to what He wants to provide and has provided, but it cannot be received without trust. Our faith in Him opens the doors for us to receive all that He has given. It is already so, in that the answers to our prayers are already in process. It is our faith that allows the answer to be received into our possession.

We are told in Hebrews 11:3, "by faith we understand that the worlds were made…" It is faith that allows us the insight to a great fact: God created the world out of nothing. Every time we view this world, we should be reminded that the same power that God used to make the world He uses to provide for His children. It is this same power God uses to feed the birds, all the birds since the beginning of time. It is the same power He uses to meet our needs when we trust Him. Not that it would take any more power, but the results are greater for us than the birds because we are His kin. We are His redeemed children and heirs to His promises. If we could have somehow watched God call the world into existence out of nothing, it might prove to be simpler for us to believe all that He is and says. However, when we believe without seeing, it is a matter of greater faith, and that pleases God.

I can remember reading in the Bible where God would account a person's faith for righteousness. This is a true teaching from this book: faith gives us the power to be counted as righteous. When we are accounted as righteous, we have access to all that God is. We will not desire to obtain and hold as our own anything that is offensive to God, and God cannot withhold anything we ask in faith because He has promised to provide for our needs. He cannot lie.

In verse six of Hebrews, chapter eleven, God says, "But without faith it is impossible to please him: for he that comes to God must believe that he is, and that he is rewarder of them that diligently seek him." Please note and remember that without faith, you cannot please God. God does not feed and shelter the worldly, halfhearted, non-committed person who goes through his Sunday routine but lives in and for the world the rest of the week. He provides for those who believe that He is, and the Bible says He will pay dividends to those who seek after Him diligently. That is the living hope that Peter wrote about in 1 Peter 1:3-5. That is the trust I have been writing about. That is the power and promise of the One who is "able to do exceedingly abundantly above all that we think or ask" (Ephesians 3:20).

Faith plays a mighty important role in all our thoughts about eternity. I take nothing away from that spiritual fact. However, faith plays a much larger role in our day-to-day living than most believers seem to think. That concerns me greatly because it is in our daily living that we need to remind ourselves that He is expecting us to trust Him exclusively.

There is an aspect of faith that we should consider very strongly. It is the area of commitment. No doubt commitment plays a vital role in our faith. Each time we utilize our faith, our commitment to Him becomes stronger. Example: When we believed on the Lord Jesus Christ for salvation, we made a commitment to trust Him with our eternal destiny. We believe He will take us to heaven for eternity when life here is over. That is a commitment. However, when commitment is made without true faith, it is nothing to God. It will require nothing of Him in response. When we wish to use our faith in God for healing or any other need, we will always be faced with making a commitment. Our effort must align with our request and God's will.

Faith in God is more than just speaking words. Commitment alone will not move God to do anything. Faith with commitment will reveal to God a trust that will gain His attention. Trust is the combination of mind and heart in a direction that pleases God and fulfills His purpose in our life. It is the effort of a believer to make something happen in heaven. All too often, we are engaged in attempting to move God to doing something on earth. It is one example of forgetting that we are His servants.

It is an honor to be able to serve Him and His kingdom and to know that we are a part of His great work. When we acquire the true heart of a servant and no longer want to be the one in charge of everything, we will begin to enjoy being His child and enjoy allowing the rest of the world to see the warm, loving heart of a humble child. Remember the Lord's teaching: "The last shall be first, and the first shall be last," and, "The least shall be the greatest; if any of you would want to be the greatest, let him become the servant of all" (Matthew 9:35).

Matthew 13:22 says, "He also that received seed among the thorns is he that hears the word of God, and the care of this world, and the deceitfulness of riches, choke out the word and he becomes unfruitful." The implication is made here that God intends for us to be fruitful, but we are hindered in our efforts to do so because of worrying and the deceitfulness of riches. God's peace and worry cannot coexist in our hearts and minds. I fear that far too many are trying to accommodate both and allowed it to become the norm in their life. After all, most of the Christian world seems to be doing the same, so why not me? Do we think that God, being so powerful, is going to destroy all causes of worry in order for us to enjoy His leadership in our lives? The truth is just the opposite; when we destroy the cause of worry and anxiety, God will then move in with all of His peace and direction.

Most of the things we tend to worry about never come to pass. They are things that may happen in the future or things we feel we should have and don't. God is the only One who knows tomorrow, and He knows all that we will need. Should tomorrow not come on earth, think of all the worry that was in vain. Can you see that all of the tomorrows are fully out of our control? There is no way that we can secure the future apart from complete trust in Christ Jesus.

We can see someone on TV or while shopping at the store and conclude that we should look like that person and could if we put forth a certain effort. So we begin to worry about changing our appearance so we can impress someone and feel superior over others who look worse than we do. You will never be really happy until your focus is changed to what God wants from you and how God wants you to appear.

I confess that one passage of Scripture that troubled me for a long time deals with this very thought. It is Paul's writing to the Philippians, chapter four, verse eleven: "I have learned that whatever state I am in, there with to be content." How could anyone be content with all that life brings to him? If a person considers all the various involvements of his life and knows peace and success in each area, he must be the happiest man on earth. How could this be?

When digging into the verse, I found that Paul was, in fact, saying that he had made Jesus Lord over every area of his life. Knowing that Christ Jesus was in charge of his financial matters and Lord over his ministry and Lord over all his relationships with people and Lord over his health and happiness, he could say, "I am content in every area of my life." We can say the same once we have given every part of our life over to the Lordship of Christ Jesus. Why should we worry about any of it if, in fact, our Lord is in charge of all?

All too often, we allow the situations of life to take charge of us rather than allowing Jesus to take charge of the situations. This is why I feel we have insulted our Master when He sees us worrying so much over the things that He has offered His personal attention to. The negative is sure to come to each of us, but when we are trusting Him—and the record is clear that trusting Him has proven to put us at ease and even heal broken hearts and find a comfortable end to grief and sorrow—we can say our focus has changed for the better.

Look long enough and hard enough at the world around you, and you will see so many things that are upsetting and fearful. You can conclude in the flesh that there is plenty for everyone to worry about. When you see these things but lift your eyes and heart to God, you will see that all the world is not big enough to disrupt His plan and His order for our lives. You can focus on the storms of life, or you can focus on the Savior. The fact about your attitude depends on which one you are looking to.

In every office at work or every class at school and in every walk of life, there are those situations that will cause us to feel vulnerable or inadequate. If we don't find them in our personal life, we can find them in our social life. If we don't find them in our physical life, we will find them in our spiritual life. We will think of disease or death or both. We will consider poverty and the loss of the ability to meet our financial obligations. There are many, many different helps available to us to help us understand what is wrong, and understanding, at least in part, can bring a certain sense of control that allows us to see where we goofed up. However, there is only one cure for this problem of worry, and that is to fully trust the God who made us, loves us, and has promised to provide all we need to live and be happy here and to take us home to heaven when we are finished here.

I encourage you to not be wimpy when it comes to facing the facts. Don't roll up all the anxiety and worry in your life and throw it at the Lord and say, "Here it is; now take care of it." Look at your situation and realize what it is that you have failed to do. Look at the promises of the Lord, realizing that He has never failed, and simply work your way through each situation until you have fully placed your complete life in His care. As

Peter says it, "Cast all your cares on Jesus, for He cares for you" (1 Peter 5:7).

I know many will want to take issue with me on the following statement, but I do believe the promises of God are to His faithful children. If we are to enjoy the fullness of His promises, we must be well read in the Scriptures, we must enjoy a meaningful prayer life, we must be aware of the way our Lord dealt with similar situations in His time on earth, and we must know what situations to confront in faith and which ones to simply let go of. There was, at one time, a common saying among Christians: "Let go and let God." That was the encouragement to let some things go, things that were too big for us or things that would prove too costly for us to approach, things that only God could deal with anyway.

Every organ in your body is caring out its functions by the design and power of God Himself. Job said it so very well in Job 34:14-15, "If He should determine to do so; if He should gather to Himself His spirit and His breath, All flesh would perish together, and man would return to dust." Remember, it is God who is keeping us alive, providing what we need, and doing it with grace and mercy. There is no need for us to be wrestling with worry and anxiety. Let Him have His way.

I watched a crew of men working in South Carolina one day in the grain fields. Huge combines were gathering the grain into large trucks, ton after ton of grain being harvested out of one field of a thousand acres or more. I have since thought back to that grain field and wondered how many such fields there were around the nation, and even around the world, and not one of them owned by a bird. Yet all the grain fields of the world would not be grain enough to feed what the Lord has fed over the years. He says to each of us, "Look at all the birds I have fed, and there is not one of them skinny or thin and not one of them dying from lack of nutrition. Are you not worth more than many birds?"

Many of the worries we have come through have proven to be untrue, just imagined troubles that never materialized at all. Most of those worries were about our future, an area of life where we have no control at all. We can say we have One who can control our tomorrows, but we have failed to trust Him. Do we not believe all that He has said in His word? Promises like Philippians 4:19, "But my God shall supply all your need according to His riches in glory, through Christ Jesus." Food and shelter are two items we need. Jesus said, "Let Me supply them for you." Do you trust Him?

We need to move to the second of the three examples the Lord gave to us in Matthew 6:25-34: "Do not worry about your stature." Now that we have seen the foolishness of worrying about food and shelter, let us look into this thought and learn still more as we reach for the life that is worry-free.

Why Worry About Our Body?

"Which of you by being anxious can add one cubit unto his stature?" (Matthew 6:27)

The word *stature* (*helikian*) means height, quality of life, or status gained by growth, or sometimes it could be used to mean age. The word *cubit* (*pechus*) literally means measure of space or distance (approximately eighteen inches), but it can also mean a measure of time or age. In the old Hebrew economy, a cubit was the distance between a man's elbow and the end of his middle finger. The distance would vary between eighteen and twenty-two inches but was most commonly near eighteen inches, and that became the norm.

We could read the verse before us as, "Who can add one cubit to his stature or one minute to his span of life?" The application is very simple but very strongly stated by the Master: It is senseless to think about adding to your height, and it is senseless to think about adding time to the length of your life. The statement puts forth a challenge, resulting in a conclusion. If you can change your stature or add to the length of your life, go ahead and do so. If you can't, then stop worrying about it.

Our Lord continues to expound on the subject of our need to trust Him. He presents the matter in three areas of life: 1) shelter, 2) stature and/or length of life, and 3) clothes. In this area of stature and/or length of life, He raises the question in such a way that we are required to consider the reality of being able to do this or not. It is rather obvious that it would be impossible for any of us to accomplish the task. It appears that He would have us see the foolishness of even thinking about such an exercise but nonetheless reach the conclusion that the alternative is simple but complete trust in Him, leaving all the impossible tasks for man to the hands of God, who can do all things.

Have any of you noticed how great an industry has grown out of cosmetics, herbal medicines, gyms, and exercise equipment? I am not speaking against the proper use of women's makeup. My grandfather used to say, "A little paint would help even the worst old barn." Then he would always excuse my grandmother from his remarks and say, "But my baby doesn't need any paint." I don't know if the Lord had any of the things I want to say in mind when He gave these verses, but it would seem appropriate.

I read in a news article that sun-tanning machines used indoors for tanning the skin are considered by the medical field to be as addictive as most other addictions, other than the stronger drugs. There seems to be a drive in most of the civilized world for men and women to change their appearance. I wonder if there is anyone who is completely satisfied with how they look. Many of the dark-skinned people want their skin to be lighter. The fair-skinned people think darker is better and will expose themselves to dangerous levels of sun or sun-tanning machines in an effort to achieve that darker look. The short want to be taller, and the taller wish they were shorter, except for a few basketball players. They will wait until their career is over in basketball before they start worrying about being too tall. The thin want a few extra pounds, and those of us with too much midriff wish for a thinner look. The dark-haired ladies want to be blonde, and the gray and white-haired men and women wish they were still dark-haired. The very young wish for an older age, and the aged spend most of their day remembering how it was when they were young.

I noticed a lady at church one Sunday morning with the most unusual color of eyes. I believe it was violet or close to violet. She was a rather lovely lady, mother of three, and had a husband who was very protective of all in his family. Knowing this, I made sure he was beside me when I asked her the question. Trying to be positive, I made it a rhetorical statement: "That is the most unusual color of eyes I have ever seen. Have your eyes always been this color?"

Her answer was, "Only about six weeks. I just got these new contacts about six weeks ago."

Now I don't want to admit my ignorance, but at that time, I did not know you could change the color of your eyes by using contact lenses. I may have appeared a bit backwoods. I believe my wife was embarrassed for me instead of embarrassed by me.

Plastic surgery has grown into a multibillion dollar industry, and most of it is not to correct birth defects or correcting damage as the result of an accident but rather allowing people to change what they do not like about their appearance. Much of the dislike is the result of the Hollywood effect. We see someone on the big screen at the theater, on the TV at home, in a magazine, or on some billboard ad, and we conclude, "I could look like that if…" The imagination takes over, and away we go.

I heard a story of a lady in the hospital who was worried about dying. She had a visit with God in prayer and was assured by God that she was not dying and in fact would live another forty years. After the prayer, she began to think about having another forty years to live. Looking in the mirror, she realized her hair really needed to be fixed. She thought while they were washing and styling her hair, she could get it colored blonde. *While I am at it,* she thought, *I could have a facelift while I am here.* A bit later in the day, she decided to have a tummy tuck, some implants, and a little Botox for the lips. Six weeks later, while leaving the hospital, she was run over by a truck and died. Arriving at the gates of heaven, she saw the Lord and summoned Him over.

She began to deride Him with the words, "You lied to me. You said I would live forty more years, and here I am just six weeks later."

The Lord came closer and looked ever so close at her and said, "Is that you, Martha? I didn't recognize you."

The point the Lord is making in our verse from Matthew is He has made us for His purpose and His glory. Whatever that plan of His is, it required us to be made the way He has formed us. Now keep in mind, please, there are many who have had their appearance altered by disease or accident, and that is a different matter to consider; repair for that which was lost or damaged by accident or disease I am sure would be approved by the Lord Himself. I, for one, believe the skill God gives the doctors is His way of making the needed repairs. However, to misuse those skills only to make money at the expense of someone wanting to look like someone else could not be right.

I remember preaching many years ago on the Ten Commandments and dealing with the law of God on the subject of "making no graven images." Part of God's displeasure was in the fact that Israel was taking that which God had made and remaking it into some other form, as if to say, "Let us improve this stone or this piece of wood." All that God made was for His purpose, and it was made perfect according to His will. We have lost all concept of that today. It is as though all that God has given us is here for us to remake or change the fashion of to suit us. Does it ever pass through our minds that some things God made He wants left alone? It would be very difficult, if not impossible, for man to know all of the things God would have us leave alone without His direction. It appears most of the time that man pushes ahead of God without even considering what he is doing.

I met an older man in Haifa, Israel, who explained to me the responsibility he had as the elder of his family. Among the many duties, one was to pick the mate for his children and grandchildren to marry. It was a very careful selection process but resulting, he believed, in finding the soul mate for each one. He believed that when God created all that is, He made everybody that was to ever be, and He made them in pairs. The elder was given the ability to know who was made for each child. He said this process would never work in America.

"Want to know why?" he asked. "Let's suppose that God made my son with a desire to know a young lady with dark hair and dark eyes and a shy kind of smile that would set her apart from other girls." He continued, "In America, when she came along and met my son, her heart would begin beating fast, and her desire for him would be very great. But he would not look the second time at her because she had colored her hair blonde and [was] acting like someone other than herself. My boy would not know she is his soul mate and pass her by. He would end up getting married to someone else and probably divorced before he is twenty."

The old man made good sense to me. We need to be more honest as to who we are and what we really would look like without all the additions. It may not be the outward appearance so much as it is the change that seems to take place within us when we pretend on the outside. Is it possible that for some the pretense continues on into years to come, making the person inside uncomfortable or misguided? Children being raised in an environment that suggests it doesn't matter what you do as long as you have a good time will surely have difficultly knowing who they are and what it is God has in store for them. Our outward man is just as much God-made as the inward man. That is, as long as we take care of ourselves and do not allow our appearance to change into something gross.

Lack of good health is a major reason for some to worry. If the poor health is not the result of the person's own abuse, the person should seek God's healing and believe He intended for us to "be of good health, and prosper, even as our soul prospers" (3 John 2). If He chooses not to heal the person, He will surely give grace sufficient to bear sickness, helping the person to see that He has a purpose and a plan to use the sickness for someone's growth and/or strength.

There are so many things in life that could be better and would be better if we would only learn to focus on the eternal purpose of God and not on our daily problems. It is as if we are the only person on earth with a burden or a problem and the only one with a need. We should be ashamed. God is in the process of carrying out His plan and purpose for time and eternity, and He has allowed you and me to be a part of the program. If you do not have a starring role, do not be discouraged; neither do I, and neither do billions of others. There is no requirement that we must be the star of the show or pout for feeling less than someone else. If we are born again, we are in the role He intended for us to play. He has provided all we need to be successful in that role, and if we do what He has asked of us, we are successful with no need to worry.

We must remember too that the afflictions we bear may be for the benefit of someone else. There may be a family member, a friend, or loved one watching our distress with great interest, and God could be using our suffering to teach and/or enrich the life of the other person or persons. I can remember tragedies in our church families that seemed to bring most of the families in the fellowship to their knees. I know there are some, even in the family of God, that would not be willing to suffer in order for others to be made stronger or even to bring a soul to Christ for salvation. We should all be willing to spend or be spent for the edification of our fellow man. I do not know where I got this saying, but I have kept it in my Bible for many years and love to read it:

> He may put thorns in you that no prayer can extract.
> Thorns that will poison and pain.
> But the thorn will enrich grace, increase humility, and make
> Weakness strong and glorious.
> Satan's thorn will change distresses and persecutions into the most divine
> pleasure.

Are we willing to suffer such a thorn that God could make us stronger and wiser? Would we be willing to suffer such pain if we knew that it was for the good of someone else, maybe someone we didn't even know? Do you think your faith could be a bit stronger? Perhaps you know someone going through some difficult times, with great need, who seems to be at the end of their wit. Would you be willing for God to use you and/or your possessions to relieve that need?

There is no better time to tell someone about God's love and saving grace than when you are helping them deal with a situation that seems to them to be beyond fixing. A good gospel sermon can do a lot of good and give some encouragement that for the moment seems so very special. However, a good sermon lived instead of preached, demonstrated by action, and one that involves the person providing the ministry suffering personal loss and/or pain will last a lot longer and prove as effective, if not more effective.

I intend to deal with a few of the examples of faith we find in Hebrews 11, but for the moment, I would like to address a very special thought from those verses. "And these all, having received witness through faith received not the promise, God having provided some better thing for us, that they without us should not be made perfect" (Hebrews 11:39-40). There were many, many people that lived hoping to see the salvation of the Lord but died before Calvary. All they had was the display of faith, both their own and the faith of others. Even though they did not see the Lord's birth, life, and death, they believed. Even though they did not see the resurrection, they believed it would take place, and they believed it told of great things to come. They had received witness through faith but received not the promise, that is, the fulfilled promise.

Now note please that the Scriptures teach that God had something better for them. Their faith, based on God's word only, was counted for righteousness. We, today, can look back and see that Christ did come to earth as a babe. He did die on the cross and was buried in a borrowed tomb but rose again on the third day. We have His messages preached and the record of His life and ministry, but they only had His promise. The point here is God's promise is always true, and it is always sufficient. What He has made us to be will be just right for His purpose. God makes no mistakes. What He has made us to be is for His pleasure and purpose.

Is it not strange that we are so able to believe God for the greater matters, such as salvation, but not the lesser matters, like daily provisions? Could it be that we are insisting that we be a part of the process? We want to take credit for and receive praise for having the ability to provide for our families and ourselves. It sounds like an ego problem or a matter of pride, allowing us to appear in the eyes of those around us as self-sufficient. If you are so inclined to believe, why not prove it to yourself and the rest of the world? All you need to do is add to your stature one cubit or, when it is time for you to die, hold up your hand, tell everyone to stop whatever they are attempting to do to help you, and say, "I will now add to the length of my life." If you succeed, all will take notice, and you can boast with all the pride you have. The simple truth is, none of us can do either. The point our Lord is making is very clear; man cannot alter these facts of life. He is saying, "Can't you see the need to trust me?"

There is another example of explicit trust in John's gospel, chapter eleven. Lazarus, a friend of Jesus and brother to Martha and Mary, had died. He is identified in his relationship to Jesus when the sisters sent word to the Master, telling Him, "The one you loved is sick." Jesus waited for two more days before He announced that He was going to Judea again. He declared that He was glad for their sakes that He was not with Lazarus because He wanted their faith to increase.

Christ had been an unwelcome guest in most of the homes of that day. His teaching was considered by many to be so radical most were afraid to be associated with Him for fear of imprisonment or death. Jesus loved this family individually and expressed His love by speaking of and to each one in the house. Everyone here was dealing with death, except the Lord. He understood death, was not afraid because of death, and was not concerned about losing His dear friend Lazarus. His motive here was the teaching of all that were present that He was the Son of God and that He had power over life and death and was to be trusted in all situations.

It seems in all of life's crises that we are tempted to rush ahead of God as fast as we can. All we can think about is getting beyond the need, counting the cost, and getting on with our life. Jesus is teaching that we need to slow down, stop worrying, and learn what the situation can teach us by trusting Him fully.

It can be so hard at times to wait on the Lord. God does not move on our time schedule, nor does He get bent all out of shape with each crisis that pops up in our life. The simple reason is He is in charge. I have been asked so many times, "Could the Lord not have prevented Lazarus's death?" The answer is very simple: yes. However, had He prevented Him dying, He would not have been able to teach such a powerful lesson to the people He loved so much. It is obvious that He placed more emphasis on the strength of His teaching and the need to trust Him than He placed on the emotions of His dear friends.

Now get this straight and very clear: Jesus will not cause sickness and death to come on a member of His family. He will, however, allow it so that He may prove a lesson that we are in need of. We may not be aware of our need for the lesson, but He knows what we need. His provision is always an effort to fulfill our need in such a way for us to be taught again and again that He is the provider and we can trust Him.

Remember when Jesus rebuked His mother when she sent Him to find more wine for the marriage feast? She was interfering with His work, His purpose for being there. Mary was there for the wedding. Jesus was there for the great lesson He was about to teach. We cannot control God's timing, nor can we control His purpose.

When we rise to living above worry, we can see the love of God, allowing us to experience heartbreak and even anger in order for us to grow closer to Him and deeper in our faith. Martha was a lady of faith, but her faith was not a complete trust in Jesus. She expressed her faith to the Master and even suggested that He could have prevented this scene had He been there. He could have healed Lazarus. She then adds a strong expression of faith by saying, "But I know that even now, whatsoever you will ask of God, God will give it to you" (verse 22). The great error here is not in a lack of faith in Christ Jesus but faith that stopped short of trusting Him as the Almighty God. Look again at the words she uses. She is placing Christ a little lower than God and suggesting that He (Jesus) would ask God for His help in the matter.

If you will look back at verse fifteen of John 11, you will hear Jesus tell the disciples what was in this experience for them. He said, "I am glad for your sakes that I was not there, to the intent you may believe; nevertheless let us go to him." The disciples believed that Jesus was the Savior sent by God. They had forsaken all else to follow Him, and yet the Master tells them something is lacking in their faith. Surely they possessed the fundamental faith that most followers of Christ have today. Jesus was referring to the ascending kind of faith I want us to see, enabling us to rise above worry and anxiety and live the life of faith that allows Christ Jesus to truly meet our needs and allows us to walk in unity with Him. He wanted His disciples to see Him in action as God, restoring life and giving peace. If you do not have this type of faith, you cannot overrule worry, and you cannot shut the door on anxiety.

Christ is God and is trying to reveal this great truth to the people gathered there at the grave of Lazarus. This is the great lesson of trusting in God. He is everything we need and will provide everything we will ever need, if we will see Him as the Almighty God who loves us with an everlasting love, a God who wants only what is best for us and will provide or withhold anything in order to teach us about His love and care for us.

Christ's answer to Martha is as much for us today as it was for her on that day. Jesus answered and said, "I am the resurrection and the life, he that believeth in me though he were dead, yet shall he live." Jesus is saying, "I am the source of all life. I am here now, and all that is available to you is standing here before you."

Jesus also says in John 11:26, "And whosoever liveth and believeth in me shall never die. Believest thou this?" When the children of God come to the end of this life, we do not die; we just relocate. In a measure of time that is less than the twinkling of the eye, we are moved from life on earth to life in heaven in the presence of God, fully alive all the way. For those of us who have trusted Christ Jesus as our Savior and Lord, death is dead. It no longer exists for us to experience. Our only dealing with death is dealing with the remains of those who die. Knowing Jesus as the resurrection and life means we know He is alive right now and with us wherever we are and whatever we are doing. He is here in the person of the Holy Spirit, in us, and all around us. Our faith is alive, and we are in continual communion with and in fellowship with Him.

The remarks of the Lord Jesus seem to have excited Martha's heart and faith to a new and higher level than before. She confessed that she believed that He was the Christ, the Son of God that was to come into the world. The peace was so great in Martha and the excitement so strong that she ran to tell Mary that the Master was come and had asked for her. The Master (*ho didaskalos*) means the teacher. The definite article *the* is important here. Jesus was and is not just another teacher. He is the Lord, the greatest of all teachers. He stands alone in this highly defined position of the greatest teacher to ever live, the Master Teacher. When Mary heard these words, she responded quickly and came to where Jesus was. I am not sure what was in Mary's mind at this time, but whatever it was created great excitement in her. She came with anticipation and expectation, somehow believing that the presence of Jesus would make a difference.

Arriving at the tomb, we are told by the Scriptures that she fell at His feet and worshipped Him. Her brother was dead. She had anticipated Jesus coming before his death to heal him. Her sister Martha was distraught and grieving. There were a great number of friends and family with them, and her heart was full of sorrow. But the first thing on her mind was to worship Jesus. I suppose it is fair to say that most of these people were grieved, concerned, some broken and troubled. The heaviest heart present was that of Jesus. The scripture states that He "was troubled" (*etaraxe heauton*), meaning emotionally moved or stirred; in fact, He was bearing the sorrow and stress of all who were there. Not only the human sorrow of each heart, but He alone was aware of the need in each life and the great distance between where they were as followers and where they could be if they would just trust Him.

Try to think with me as to how the Lord saw the crowd of mourners gathered to show their love and concern for Martha and Mary. No doubt some of them were related to Lazarus and his sisters. They were there to express their sorrow for the loss of Lazarus. I feel comfortable in saying not one of them saw the purpose of God. None could see the Master's desire for them to know Him as God, the Almighty God, with a plan to use this situation as a tool to teach them a very, very important lesson. The lesson is simply this: Christ Jesus is God, and whenever He is involved in our life, there is no real loss. The human pain we feel, the fear that may flood our mind, the sick feeling in the pit of our stomach are all allowed so that we might see the intensity of the lesson that is being presented to us. If the Master is there and we know He is there with us, how can we not trust Him with whatever the cost of the lesson? He has promised to work all things together for our good; He has promised to never leave us nor forsake us; we know we are to live with Him in eternity. How can we fail to realize that even in life's most demanding crises, we are still winners because of His love? There is no need to worry!

In Hebrews 11:6, the Bible says, "But without faith it is impossible to please him; for he that cometh to God must believe that he is, and that he is a rewarder of them that diligently seek him." The little word *is* needs to be considered. It is in the present tense, indicating that we must believe that He is here with us, as close as our own breath, when we call on Him. If you are praying to a God in the distant heavens and trying to pray through all the trouble and mess of life and pray around all the TV preachers, you may never get an answer to your prayer. Pray, however, to the God who is as near as the words in your mouth, believing that He is so near because of His love for you and your faith in Him, and the answer will come. If He must say no to your request, understanding will help you see why the request was denied. Perhaps the request was not denied at all but delayed until a more appropriate time. Being able to accept God's timing may sometimes require as much faith as any other prayer we pose to Him.

Faith must be focused on Him. He is the source of what we are asking for. He is the reason for request. If we cannot justify our request by His will, chances are very slim that we will see the answer given. Faith is not receiving from God what we asked but accepting what He gives. The character of the Christian is ordered by God's providence. It is when we become anxious about what lies beyond the providence of God that our faith waivers and we become spiritually weak.

Most of the New Testament deals with the life of a believer in the time frame of one day. "This is the day the Lord has made, let us rejoice and be glad in it." The thought I get from this verse is this day is all we have. Yesterday is gone, and tomorrow has not yet been made. Have you ever thought, *What if I spend all day worrying about tomorrow and tomorrow doesn't come?* or, *I might die before today ends.* Then all of the worry was in vain. What a waste of time and energy.

How many days have we had that we allowed worry to destroy God's intended purpose for us? That which was intended for us to accomplish was not done: the ministry, the work, the worship, the praise, the time in prayer. None of it was done because we were too busy worrying, and all for nothing. If you can change your stature or if you can add to your life one day, go ahead and worry; you are the exception to God's Word. If you cannot make such additions to your life, stop worrying about it. Leave it alone, and allow God to do as it pleases Him to do.

The key to having a successful day is to do only that which is part of this day. Do not complicate it by trying to do today what needs to be done tomorrow. Stay focused on today, asking God to order your steps. If God is walking with you each step of the way, as He promised He would do, why should you spend one moment in worry?

I see in the Bible God's purpose to keep His children happy. He wishes for each of us to know the joy of living with Him in us and all around us. Oh, the negative things we allow or bring into our life, knowing He is present with us. We must guard against the spirit of distrust. No matter what Satan tempts us with, no matter what may be happening in the life of one near and/or dear to us, stay focused on God's love and purpose. He does not wish any evil to overtake us, and we can know peace even when the storm is raging.

Do not become as one who fights the distortion of our future. Satan can cause us to imagine all sorts of things that might happen tomorrow, and that can result in our spending days worrying for nothing, just imaginations playing with our mind and proposing all sorts of difficulties that do not exist. When we spend time dealing with the things that could go wrong tomorrow, we are wasting our energy and time. The option is to trust Him for tomorrow and walk with Him today.

Where is our faith when we are living in fear of tomorrow? How can we express faith in the Lord Jesus, believing that He is here with us now, today, and all day long, when we are worried about tomorrow? What about today?

Look around you at the world from God's point of view. Do not focus on the negative, on all the destruction caused by Satan and his company of non-believers. God's power is made manifest all around us in creation and the preservation of all that He has made. Watch the sun rise and know that He is near, in all of His power and glory. See the world as the handiwork of His hands and know that His prized position is man and all that He has made is for man to enjoy and to learn to use for His glory and honor. When we see the handiwork of God, it should remind us that He is still in control, and we can commit any and all of our situations to His care.

Worry can only be enforced when faith is asleep. When we practice ascending faith, fully trusting Him and believing He is with us now, no matter the situation, we will not, cannot, worry. There is a divine providence directing the course of the world. We can live in harmony with God's plan, or we can go contrary to it. Walking with Him is joy. Walking contrary to Him is worry, fear, and doubt. With Him, we have peace that passes understanding; without Him, we have ulcers, sleepless nights, premature aging, and a whole list of other problems that none of us want. Within the family circle, it will only take one person to worry enough to spoil everything for the rest of the family. When we learn to live above worry, using the ascending kind of faith, we will enjoy His presence with us, knowing that the world cannot disrupt our fellowship. I believe that God would stop the efforts of the whole world in order to prove Himself faithful to one of His children who was fully trusting in His love. God cannot fail. It isn't a matter of us doing enough to merit His favor or a matter of how much time we spend in prayer. This will blow the mind of some of our Christian family, but God is not so much concerned with how often we worship and how much we put in the offering plates but when we fully trust Him and His word. I have heard it said so many times that if I had only done this or that, He would have answered my prayer. Oh, dear friend, please hear me. God is watching to see how much faith we have in Him. Do you trust Him fully and without reserve?

James said in his epistle, "You have not because you ask not, and you ask and receive not, because you ask amiss, that you may consume it on your own lust" (James 4:2-3). This is so simple to understand; if you do not ask, why would God be motivated to give to you? If you ask for your own pleasure without considering what God wants, why would He give to you, knowing you will waste it on yourself in seeking pleasure?

The advice given us by the Lord Jesus in James 4:8 is, "Draw near to God, and He will draw near to you. Cleanse your hands, ye sinners and purify hearts, ye double minded." How do we draw near to God in order to receive His blessings and His fellowship? We cleanse our hands—that is how we treat our fellow man—and we purify our hearts—that is how we think and feel toward each other. How many times have you heard someone say in defense of themselves, "Well, God knows my heart."? That is a way of saying, "I know I did wrong, but you don't know it and could not know it, so I pretend that God knows my thoughts and is pleased with me."

Please consider this carefully; God does know our hearts! It is what He sees and knows that keeps us from receiving His blessings and His help. Our motives are wrong if we are not living in the ascending level of faith that allows for fellowship and communication between God and us.

God is concerned with how much faith we have in Him and how much we trust Him in every area of life. Our time on earth is not for the joy of living a carefree, happy life, fulfilling the desires of the flesh and dying a rich old man/woman. Our time on earth is for the purpose of serving God, finding a purpose in clean holy living, and a ministry that allows us to serve Him every day in some way. Then when we leave this world for eternity, we will be equipped to really live and enjoy a never-ending life in service to Him. When we compare the length of life here with the length of life there, it seems so foolish to ever worry about anything here on earth. If your lifespan on earth was a thousand years and you found a way to gather more money than anyone else on earth and died without God in your life and had never given your heart to Him, you would die a miserable person, lonely and afraid. One second in eternity, and you would be willing to give up all your wealth and all one thousand years of life if you could escape the eternity awaiting you and beg God to come into your heart. But it cannot be done.

Remember the rich man and Lazarus in Luke 16:19-31? Both characters in this passage had died. One had gone to heaven, the other to hell. The one in hell cried out for mercy after he had sinned away all the days of mercy, too busy spending his money and buying pleasure for his flesh to have time for God. The Bible says in verses twenty-three to twenty-four, "In Hades he lifted up his eyes, being in torments, and seeth Abraham afar off, and Lazarus in his bosom. And he cried and said, 'Father Abraham, have mercy on me, and send Lazarus that he may dip the tip of his finger in water, and cool my tongue; for I am tormented in this flame.'" All the years of living with the luxuries of life suddenly lost their appeal. He was now willing to trade it all for one drop of water, even if it was delivered on the tip of the beggar's finger. What a sad realization when one sees the brevity of life when compared to eternity. Add to the scene the difference between eternity without God and eternity with God, and you will begin to see the advantage of serving God now and living with Him forever. No amount of money can buy that joy, and no life on earth can be lived so lavishly that it could ever be compared to life in heaven.

The rich man was reminded that while on earth he had had his good things and Lazarus had received evil things, but now Lazarus was comforted and the rich man was tormented. The great gulf between the two men was fixed by God. No one could leave the torment of Hades and find a way to get into heaven.

Neither is it possible for one to leave heaven to cross over that great gulf into Hades. The teaching is that the choice we make here about eternity is not changeable. It is fixed for a never-ending eternity. The decision requires each of us to make sure we are living the life God has asked of us. There is no going back after life is over.

If there were no life after death, if there were no heaven to gain or hell to shun, I would still want to live the life of a Christian. The one most important part of my life is having Jesus for a Friend; having His presence with me and His Word to teach me and His Spirit to guide me is better than anything I know. My sins are forgiven, and when I fail to keep His words, I find Him leading me back to the truth and offering forgiveness and cleansing. This allows me to live with confidence and joy, day after day, knowing that when life is over here on earth, I have missed nothing of value, lost nothing of importance, and have the best ever offered man waiting for me before the next heartbeat. When trials and difficult moments come, I have no need to panic, no need to fear, no loss of sleep, and no anxiety because He has promised to take care of me, and I believe He will keep His word.

For me, the best part of being a Christian is very personal. It has nothing to do with any other believer's experience, nothing to do with all the hope and joy I have about the future; it has more to do with the daily joy I experience in walking with Him, talking with Him, and finding His counsel, forgiveness, and love so very personal and rewarding. I will not trade what I have in my relationship with Jesus for a million worlds and what they may hold. Christ Jesus has given me a peace that cannot be bought or sold, a purpose that cannot be denied nor ignored, and a hope (God's permission to expect) that will not go away. Why should I worry? Why would men think any effort to intimidate me would cause one moment of worry or fear? Why worry or wonder about anything in the world when my future is forever settled in heaven?

When these old bodies begin to act up or fail to perform correctly, there is no need to worry about it. Simply trust the One who designed it to make the necessary corrections via doctor, hospital, or all by Himself, and go on with life as normal, believing there is a divine purpose in all that happens and He has promised to never fail us. Do not place too much emphasis on the problem, but try to focus on the lesson being taught and how to benefit from the whole experience. He is there every time and knows what He is doing or allowing to be done and has a plan to use it for our good and His glory. If we have trusted Him with our salvation (the greater issue), why not trust Him with the lesser issues of life? How could we be so blind to think that He would provide the greater needs and then deny us the lesser things we need? His provision is the same in proportion as His love. Stop for a moment and think about all that we have and enjoy because of His love for us. With that in mind, think about all that He is willing to do for us because of the same love.

Why Worry About Clothing?

Now let me turn our thoughts to our worries about clothing.

"And why take ye thought for raiment? Consider the lilies of the field, how they grow; they toil not, neither do they spin..." (Matthew 6:28). Here is another invitation from our Lord Jesus to invest in one of His lessons. He has chosen one of earth's most beautiful flowers with design and color unmatched by any of earth's vegetation. Consider, says He, the splendor of this flower, which cannot be matched by even Solomon in all of his kingly robes. Even the gold, silver, and ivory of the king's palace cannot compare with that which God has made. There are several ideas that are implied in this thought, and I want us to consider a few of them.

Even in the time of Solomon, clothing played an important role in the social life of all men and women. The price of a garment could easily be noted, allowing one's position in society to be recognized immediately. The color, as well as the price of the materials, indicated the station in life as well as certain responsibilities the person might have.

Jesus said the lilies do not toil nor spin. That is to say, they do not labor for clothing or design; neither do they sit at a spinning wheel, endeavoring to create a garment or an appearance. God is saying, "I feed the birds, I decide the stature and length of a man's life, and I will clothe the lilies, and if I will do this for birds and flowers, do you not know I will do it and more for you, not in some thrown-together fashion, but to the best of My ability?" This all has to do with God's view of things. God feeding the birds may not make much of an impression on some people. God having the final say-so in the length of our life on earth or our stature may not impress some; neither will many take notice of the fact that God decides what is beautiful in the design of a flower or the colors of a flower. But the bottom line is God has an opinion as to what looks good on you and me. He is saying, "I care how you appear to the world. Allow Me to clothe you; allow Me to make you beautiful in My eyes. Do not worry about what the world thinks; be comfortable wearing what I provide for you."

He asked us to consider the beauty of Solomon for a comparison to what He wants to do for us. Solomon lived in the most lavish lifestyle possible. In the Chronicles, we can read about the temple he built and the house where he lived. In the temple, cypress was used for the wood and was overlaid with fine gold. There were ornamental palms and chains, precious stones. It wasn't just any gold but the gold of Parvaim, which, after refining, possessed a slight pink tint but was ever so smooth. His whole house was overlaid with gold. Inside the house, giant beams that supported the ceiling were covered in gold. The decorations on the walls were made of gold, and some walls were completely covered in gold. His throne was carved from ivory and overlaid with gold. Can you imagine the size of the ivory before being carved into the pieces of the throne?

A simple truth is found here that supports the greater fact of what God sees as being important. Ivory was then and still is today of great value, but the ivory in Solomon's throne was covered with gold. No one could see the ivory inside the gold, but God knew it was there, and Solomon knew it was there.

Goldsmiths and carvers were brought from all over the known world to create the cherubim and the instruments in the holy of holies. There were six steps leading up to the throne, with a footstool attached to the throne, all covered with gold. The arms of the chair and twelve lions, standing six on each side of the throne, were all covered with gold. All of Solomon's dishes used for eating or drinking were made of gold. So much gold was visible that silver lost its value in comparison to the gold. "For the king made silver *as common* as stones in Jerusalem" (2 Chronicles 9:17-27). God established the standard of beauty in those buildings of Solomon, and He established the standard of beauty in the adorning of the flowers of the field. He is saying to us today, "Consider the lilies of the field" (verse 30).

"If then God so clothe the grass, which is today in the field, and tomorrow is cast into the oven, how much more will he clothe you, O you of little faith?" (Luke 12:28). All these flowers are temporary; you and I are eternal. Will God not care much more for us as His children than for the grass that appears for only a short while and is gone? If God thinks the lilies are more beautiful than Solomon's entire splendor, we should give our trust to Him, believing He will clothe us with that which makes us beautiful in His eyes, as beautiful as the lilies.

Now here is a question for you to think upon: Are we willing to accept God's standard of quality and beauty when it is so radically different from the styles of Hollywood and/or the world? Whom do we trust to set the standard? Can we learn to live in the sunshine of His approval and feel beautiful in His eyes when the world is making fun of us or mocking us as fools? We are dealing with the dignity of God's nature. God has exposed His preference as to our appearance. Do we accept his preference as standard and measure ourselves in His eyes only?

I have never asked a lily or any other plant if they were comfortable, but if they could talk, I would wager they are not in any pain. I know that some of the people I see every day of my life cannot say the same. I have seen stacked heels on ladies that had to be at least six inches tall, perhaps more. There is no way on earth you can convince me that is comfortable. Some clothes are so tight it would be a struggle to breathe, and sometimes in the winter, I have seen people with not enough clothes to warm a small dog, let alone an adult. Do the lilies have more common sense than some people? Not really. They just accept a higher standard when it comes to dressing.

The life of a lily teaches us about a life without worry and care. How unselfishly they grow, with no awareness of any opinion other than the Creator who ordained all that is to please Him. The lily seeks only the reward of the Father's approval by not questioning or doubting why He made them so. Ever hear a lily wish to be a rose or a tree or a bush? Their only intent is to serve the Master's will, grow beautiful in His sight, and know the smile of His approval. Everything that has life, just as everyone who has life, enjoys that life as a gift from God. We should all realize that with the gift of life comes the responsibility. Think for just a moment how great it would be if man responded to our Creator like the lilies and other plants and trees. All of God's design is perfect in His eyes, and I am sure there is no fuss or refusal to obey from the plants and animal kingdom. As people, we can get close to obeying God, but it will take eternity before we can perfect our obedience.

Look around you; is God providing for the flowers? Are they truly beautiful? You have no need to worry; He will do even more for you. How simple He is making the lesson here. No scientific theory, no equations, just birds and flowers and simple matters like that.

We are faced with the ugly fact of denying the truth of God's Word. When we exalt ourselves to the throne of our heart and declare our goals and our desires to own so much and appear in such a manner without considering the Creator's preference, we have allowed the monster *I* to take authority in our life. Our lack of love and/or respect for the truth has driven us away from desiring to please Him to a desire of pleasing ourselves. We think that in pleasing ourselves and in winning the approval of those around us we will find our place in life and be satisfied. I don't know how much peace we can find in the praises of our fellow man, but I do know that when we are pleasing in our Master's eyes, we have peace and joy. There is no real, lasting freedom from worry and anxiety until we are free from ourselves, our flesh.

Isaiah 26:3-4 states it this way: "Thou wilt keep him in perfect peace, whose mind is stayed on thee: because he trusteth in thee. Trust in the Lord forever; for in the Lord Jehovah is everlasting strength." Here, it is stated so clearly anyone should be able to understand. If you want to live in peace, live above worry and trust in the Lord. The promise is given here in Isaiah that if we consider His will, His way, His plan, allowing our mind to stay on Him, He will do the rest. He will provide, He will protect, and He will give peace instead of worry and anxiety.

In order for me to show the seriousness of this dilemma, I will refer to a few verses in Luke 21:25-26 talking about the anxiety that is to be prevalent during the last days just before the church is taken away. He says, "And there shall be signs in the sun, and in the moon, and in the stars, and upon the earth distress of nations, with perplexity (*aporia*), the sea and the waves roaring; Men's hearts failing them for fear, and for looking after those things which are coming on the earth; for the powers of heaven shall be shaken." Now read this very closely, for there is something here we need to learn.

It appears that everything around us is pointing to the soon return of our Lord Jesus Christ. As believers, we have a pretty good idea as to the things that will be taking place just prior to His return. Without some knowledge and without sufficient faith, we would all be in a perplexed state of mind. That is the feeling of being trapped with no way out. With all the recent changes in our nation against Christianity and favoring non-Christian religions and secular humanism, laws banning public prayer for Christians but not non-Christian religions, and laws banning Christian activities and/or anything relating to Christianity, it is causing a lot of anxiety in the hearts of weak Christians and those professing to be a Christian but who have never fully learned to trust our Lord Jesus. While these hearts grow weaker, it gives place for Satan to move into their minds, sowing all kinds of deceitful ideas. It is not a difficult task to look around you in a shopping mall or on a busy street and see the difference between you as God's child and the rest of the world. Being different in our hearts results in our appearing different on the outside. Solomon tells us that "as a man thinks in his heart, so is he" (Proverbs 23:7). I must say I have seen some sights that would make us wonder what was on the inside.

There are no doubt millions today worried about the very thing Jesus was speaking about in Matthew chapter six. It is my belief that one of the main purposes of Christ's teaching in these verses about living above worry is to help us not lose sight of our goal, to remind us that we are to be delivered from all of this mess, and to give us peace while we wait for His return. We have seen the Word of God compromised by the world, but not so in the heart of the true believer. God has not forsaken us; neither can He forsake us because He has stated in His word that, "He will never leave us nor forsake us" (Hebrews 11:5). He cannot lie;

therefore, we have no need to worry about the changing times and the negative move against our faith.

It will no doubt get a lot worse before we see Him come in the clouds of glory to receive us unto Himself, but until then, we must not allow ourselves to lose our focus on Him. We must not change our priorities and begin thinking like the unsaved world. It is time to stand firm and continue to live with all the hope our hearts can hold and rest in the assurance of His Word. Never give place to worry or doubt. That can only give the devil pleasure to see us as cowards at the very moment in time that we should be stronger and surer than ever before that He will take care of us.

If you must look back for any reason, remember all the things the Lord has freed us from in our past. Remember all the things He has brought us through to get to this point and time. Stay focused on His leading, and trust Him to deliver us through whatever Satan throws at us.

Remember when Israel was fleeing from Egypt? Not many days on the way out of bondage, the children of Israel began to complain. It was too hot, there wasn't enough food, they didn't have fresh water, and some were even worrying about their clothes and shoes. When they thought back on their life in Egyptian bondage, they only remembered the food they ate and the comforts they had found being slaves. They did not think about the pain of labor and the long hours of toiling in the hot sun. Nor did they think about the fact that they were in a strange country and their labor was for their enemy. If they had paid attention to the plagues that God had sent Egypt, they would have been able to understand the lesson God was giving.

We, just like them, forget all that God has done for us when we are facing some difficult moment in our present life. How soon we forget God's goodness and His promise to provide for our needs. The truth is, the faithfulness of God demonstrated to us in our past is proof that He will do no less in our future. We have no need to worry about tomorrow because we have a past full of His blessings and love. I have worshipped many times with people of third world countries, where there were very few fashion statements. The people were thankful to be clothed, especially if they had shoes too. Wearing the same suit of clothes I wear any day here in the States caused me to feel overdressed. I learned that there was no issue with clothing in the church or in the Christian community. No one was complaining about being out of style or wearing the same old dress that they wore last year. The focus was the content of their hearts, not their clothing. Being comfortable was a matter of being fully covered, not being in style. The idea of comfort for many has changed into a fashion statement, not just being clothed. Because God loves us so much, He cares about the way we look and the way we feel about our clothing, but the focus must be on His desires toward us, more than public opinion.

I believe with all my heart that there are some people today that do not want to be freed from the past or from some sin they are enjoying. Fashions can make a statement about the character of the person wearing the clothes. It is what we feel in our hearts that determines the style of clothing we may wear. Proving themselves to be true to God would mean giving up something or someone or a style of clothes that they are embracing with a stronger hold than they ever imagined. Allowing God to truly bless them today would mean getting rid of that sin they are enjoying so much. If you read the story of the children of Israel leaving Egypt, you might think God was taking them out of Egypt against their own will. This is a perfect example of God knowing what is best for us and the need for us to fully trust Him. Learn not to focus on the situation but on the Savior.

For some four hundred years, Israel had prayed for deliverance. Now that deliverance had come, they were not so ready to make the move toward the Promised Land. Starting over can be a fearful experience. Be sure to count the cost before you begin asking God to move you into a life without worry. I have watched over the years of counseling how many individuals suffering in an abusive relationship prayed and prayed for God to make a way of escape for them. No sooner had God answered their prayer until they were involved in another relationship just as abusive as before.

It is so easy for this to happen because they feel comfortable with an abusive person. They have learned how to deal with the hard times, with the abuse. A new life without the abuse would require learning new things, developing a new way to think and respond. It is difficult for them to refocus and look beyond what is common to them and see the life God has for them. The old life became the norm, and they just settled into the routine. Abuse, and everything that goes with it, was just another day of the same old thing. Thank God for His love and that He continues seeking us out and not letting up until we see the light of His love.

I have seen those who made the choice to turn to Christ, but the first time something from the past pops up or someone from the past shows up, they fall right back into the some old mess. Then, more likely than not, they want to blame God for deserting them. It isn't God who is doing the deserting, and it isn't the person that has been deserted. It is God's intention that we live as free people in His grace. God does not want us enslaved to sin, bondage, habits, fears, worries, and anxiety, and going around talking about all our troubles, leaving the impression in the minds of the unsaved world that there is no truth of freedom and joy in serving the Lord Jesus.

Our lives are a major portion of God's advertisements. Can you imagine the message the world is getting from some of the stories you have heard? If God thought like some of us, there would be a lot more folks dying so as to put an end to the negative advertisements. Isn't grace a wonderful thing, and along with it God's mercy, without which most of us would be dead today?

Consider the lilies, how they grow. Have you ever noticed that lilies grow from deep roots? If we learn to place our roots, the basics of our faith, deeply in the things of God and in His promise to care for us, we may begin to worry less and enjoy Him more.

We are such creatures of habit and want to be self-sufficient. This is not pleasing to our Lord Jesus. He wants us to be dependent on Him, but not to the point we sit down and wait for Him to be as our slave, running errands and doing chores as if He were a robot or a maid. Life is meant to be shared with Him. He wants to be a part of our daily life and included in all the events of the day, the good things we attempt to do and the times of disappointment and failure. Rejoice in the victories, and learn from the lessons. The thought here is to help us see that how we feel has everything to do with how we appear. For the child of God, to be dressed in the finest fashion of the day but not know God's peace in our heart would cause a problem. When we are dressed in what we bought, knowing His approval should make us feel better. Our confidence level will be visible when we interface with others because of what we feel on the inside.

Try thinking like the lily. If the lily could speak and we could understand, he would no doubt say something like this: "I feel so beautiful when God looks at me." Should two lilies engage in a conversation, it might go like this: "So you see all the people looking at us? Listen to the remarks about our color and/or beauty. Don't you bet the roses are jealous of our big blooms and striking colors?" How foolish that would be. The only voice the lily would hear is that of the Creator God who made them. The only desire they would know would be His pleasure in seeing them strong, beautiful, and completely yielded to His purpose and will. So it should be with us.

We tend to place far too much importance on how others may see us or how others may think of us and not what God sees and thinks. Clothing, like all else in our lives, should not be measured in quantity, and the quality should only come into consideration as we use good judgment and common sense to get the best buy for the money spent.

I am a nut for buying only sale items. All of my clothes are bought at the end of the season when the price is reduced so the store can make room for incoming merchandise. I have several pairs of shoes in my closet that have never been out of the box they came in. Most of them are $80 to $95 shoes, but none of them cost me more than $12. Now you may call me cheap, and that is all right; I don't mind.

I don't know the number of times someone has come to my house and I noticed they needed shoes, so I gave them a pair or two pairs of my shoes. I have noticed at work that someone needed shoes, and I was pleased to bring them a pair and, when possible, not let them know where they came from. Oftentimes in traveling to third-world countries for ministry, I would pack all my bags would hold but come back without any clothes. There was such a need among the pastors and people I was working with, and my investment in clothes was not that great since I bought only sale items. That does sound cheap, now that I think of it, but it was a great joy to see the faces of people when they tried on a pair of shoes or a new suit. Is it not much more fun to give as much away as you can instead of storing up as much as you can?

I remember the Lord saying, "The foxes have holes, and the birds of the air have nest, but the Son of Man has nowhere to lay His head" (Matthew 8:20). I don't imagine He needed much of a closet to store His garments.

To be totally honest with you, I have a bit of a problem with some of our TV pastors wearing suits of the several thousand dollars variety while preaching about a Christ that did not own a change of garments and no surplus of shoes for His feet. History teaches us that He walked everywhere He went. We seem to think it looks best if the world sees us arrive on Sunday mornings in a new luxury car. When we fly, it must be first class all the way. We prefer to stay at the best hotels and eat the finest of foods. How can we relate this to the way Jesus traveled, dressed, and ate in His earthly ministry? I heard one minister say he was sure that if the Lord were here today, He would be driving the finest automobile and wearing only the best men's suit money could buy. I find that very hard to believe. Christ was so concerned about the well-being of others that I don't think He would place Himself before anyone.

Believers should not allow themselves to become consumed with laboring day after day in order to buy external adornments that are not real. What is on the outside does not reflect what is in the heart. The external is artificial at best and always superficial. We are to allow what is on the inside to shine out in honor of whose we are and what we stand for. I am not speaking of false piety or reverting to the Puritan days of overstated modesty. I do not think we must all dress alike in order to keep from one feeling less than another. It is all in allowing what is in our heart out, out without hesitation, out without fear of injury to another's conviction or standard. If that which is in our heart is pleasing to God, we have nothing to worry about. When we know for a fact that God has approved of our clothing, should someone be offended with our appearance, it is between them and God.

So do not state that God has approved your clothes if, in fact, you do not know that to be true. Your offense is not just toward man but also toward God. We do not want to be guilty of knowingly offending God. He will always get the last word, and you cannot hide when He decides to repay. God already knows what is in our hearts, and there is no way to hide the truth from Him. Our problem is in admitting the truth to ourselves.

I have watched the faces of people coming into our worship services and even in public arenas where we have done evangelistic services, and the look of their face was crying out, "Look at me; look at me." If God were there visibly, they would be hiding their face and crying, "Don't look at me; don't look at me."

I marvel at the mink coats, exotic skins, and leather garments that are often worn to God's house on Sunday. Everyone knows we go to God's house on Sunday to worship and not to be seen. Some have decided they can do both and offend no one. It is a matter of the intent of our heart and a matter or where our priority is set. If the outward appearance is foremost in your reason for attending God's house on Sunday, you should not expect a blessing but an effort on God's part to show you, through His love, the error of your way. In the public arena, we should not strive to be seductive or appear as the poster boy for Hollywood but always clean, neat, and well groomed in such a fashion that God would be pleased, and even by our neatness, the public can see we are not attempting to please them more than God. I know God looks on the heart, but that does not mean He does not care what we display on the outside.

In the very beginning of my ministry, one of my mentors called me aside one Sunday and suggested to me that I avoid starting preacher habits. "You are allowing your habits to replace the leadership of the Holy Spirit if you do." At that time, it was very common in the Southeast for preachers to loosen their necktie if they got a little warm. And if the preacher was really doing his job, he would take off his coat and lay it aside, indicating how hard he was preaching. There were all kinds of physical demonstrations that went along with the removal of the coat, like louder preaching and a wind-sucking sound that caused the face to turn either dark red or blue. Sometimes it was downright scary. Anyway, I promised my mentor I would not give in to any such habits.

Not many months after that conversation with my mentor, I was to be a part of a team of pastors that would conduct ten days of services on the island of Jamaica. I preached every night and once or twice daily, always with my coat and tie in place, in temperatures around the mid to high nineties and the humidity pretty close to the same number. I could lose weight so fast it would make Jenny Craig envious. Everyone wondered, and some even asked, why I dressed the way I did. When asked or when some statement was made, I explained my heart. I did not want anyone misunderstanding my motive for the way I dressed.

I am now working in California as a hospital chaplain. I do a lot of public speaking, both in churches and civic groups. I always wear my suit and tie or sport coat and tie, and I always have to give an answer to the questions, "Why do you dress like that?" I do not think it wrong for the pastors here to wear more casual clothes, and I do not judge them. It is between them and God, and I know God is a fair God. Nor do I expect to be judged by anyone else. What is in my heart is between me and God, and I believe God is a fair God. The point is: it is not what others think or say that should matter; it is the fact of what is in our heart toward God. His opinion is the only one that will matter when we stand before Him to give account of the deeds done in this body, whether it is good or bad. Every word and every thought must be accounted for on that day. The truth in your heart will be there, and the entire Christian world will be there. We need to get it right!

Clothing is used for protection, covering, and adornment. Look at these three applications and realize that God never intended that we make an idol out of the way we dress, nor should we use the way we dress for any purpose other than the reasonable. We must be protected from the weather and should wear clothing suitable to the weather conditions we are in, whether it be seasonal or geographical, never to the extreme but in comfort and good health. Our clothing should keep us from being exposed in public. It would be easy to say a lot more on this topic, but I am sure most of my readers will understand what is meant by this point.

Clothing is also intended for attractiveness. Please, in thinking about this, rule out seductiveness or being stylish (to the point it is vulgar) and anything that would be dangerous to your health. There has never been a generation since the beginning of time that did not dress for adornment or for attractiveness, and there will never be another generation that does not do the same. However, the One or ones whom we should be trying to impress should have a very strong priority: the Lord first, our husband or wife second, our children third, our place of employment fourth, and our church fifth. In today's economy, there would be no church as we know it if the people did not earn their living and were able to pay a tithe and offering to the church. Even in our larger churches, there would not be enough chickens and eggs or cheese to pay all the staff. I have had several people want to express their disagreement with the forth and fifth priority. Please consider the importance of support for the church today. Without vocations, the people of the church could not support the financial needs of the church.

If we are not putting the Lord first in our life, everything else in our life will be out of order. All life and every life should place God before everything and everybody else. It is when He is number one in our life that He helps us organize the others in the proper place. The husband will be a better husband when God is first in his life. The wife will be a good wife when God is first in her life. I am not talking about putting church first, not even God's Word. I am talking about allowing God to hold the highest seat of honor and respect in your life.

It is beginning to look like most of God's family on earth is living in the extreme left or the extreme right, and neither have a solid biblical foundation to stand on. Living for Christ is to fulfill the Lord's request for us to "come out from among them, and be ye separate."

Much of the confusion today with the church is leaking out from all the efforts to blend the world and worship together, to meet the expectations of both man and God and somehow find direction for living by both standards at the same time. It is an oxymoron; it cannot be done. If you are feeling any measure of success within this arrangement, you are living as a hypocrite. James calls you a double-minded person and warns that you should not expect to receive anything from God (James 1:8). In James 4:8, he shows the answer for this problem: "Draw near to God...Purify your hearts, ye double minded." Double-minded implies the person is drawn in two directions or seeking to achieve two opposing goals. It can also mean trying to live by two opposing standards. You can see how easy it would be for one to worry or be overly anxious in this state of mind.

Clothing in the workplace and in the schools has become a matter of grave concern. The idea is to dress in such a way as to be accepted or to blend in. Oftentimes that may prove to be a bit of a problem for the Christian. Not only does this result in dressing for popularity, it also lays a heavy burden on us to be concerned about what is stylish and what is fashionable. It would be terrible if someone thought we were wearing last year's fashions or something that would conflict with the style of the day. Look at this closely, and you will see the problem is dressing in order to be acceptable.

Ask yourself the question, "For whom am I dressing?" Who is it that you feel you must please with your fashion? I certainly do not believe a wife should cause her husband to worry all day because she has dressed for the day in a way that will surely attract the attention of carnal-minded men. I was asked the question many years ago, "Who commits the sin of lust when a man looks at a woman's dress in a very exposing way? Is it the man lusting or the woman who dresses just for that reason?" Is dressing in order to create lust acceptable with God?

I see the problem here as being entangled with this short-lived time on earth and forgetting the eternal matter before us. Men, like the lilies of the field, are here today and all too soon gone. There isn't time to worry about clothing or trying to impress others with our apparel. We do need to realize that God has a preference as to how we dress, or more so, for whom we dress. If we do not care nor give consideration to what the Lord thinks about our dress, we are surely in trouble.

I can hear the minds of those disagreeing with me and crying out, "The Lord does not look on the outward appearance of man. God looks on the heart." I say a strong, "Amen." He does look on the heart, and He knows the full content of the heart. It isn't that He wants to look on the outward appearance of man; He doesn't need to look on the outside because He knows our hearts. The outside does not change anything in the heart; it is merely the outward expression of what is in our hearts. What a waste of time, money, and effort.

The psalmist said in Psalm 49:14, "...And their beauty shall consume in the grave from their dwelling." Can you see the futility of beauty when there is no way for it to reach beyond the grave? If dressing to impress or seduce others is only effective for a lifetime and can only reap carnal benefits, what is the purpose? We need something that will reach beyond death and the grave. We need something that can impress God and prepare us for an eternity in His presence. That could only be a clean heart and a desire to do all we do for the glory of God, including the way we dress and the reason for which we dress the way we do. Certainly this would rule out the worry and anxiety we create by trying to keep up with the style and standards for dress seen by the world.

Need more biblical proof? How about 1 Timothy 2:9-10? "In like manner also, that women adorn themselves in modest apparel, with shamefacedness and sobriety; not with braided hair, or gold, or pearls, or costly array; but (which becometh women professing godliness) with good works." And again in 1 Peter 3:3-4:

> Whose adorning let it not be that outward adorning of plaiting the hair, and of wearing of gold, or of putting on of apparel; but let it be the hidden man of the heart, in that which is not corruptible, even the ornament of a meek and quiet spirit, which in the sight of God is of great price.

There are other scriptures that we could use, but they all say about the same thing on this subject. I would not want anyone to be overwhelmed about the matter but ready to open their heart and mind before the Lord and ask for His directions.

The family of God is not like the rest of the world. We are different. The rest of the world, the unsaved, is consumed with the affairs of this world. They know nothing other than this world's standard. Don't be too harsh on them, but do not allow them to influence you in their way of living. This is stated fairly strongly in Ephesians 2:12, 19, that those in the world are without Christ. Without the Lord Jesus living in their heart, via presence of the Holy Spirit, they cannot understand our way or our standard. While we seek to please our Lord, they live to please the flesh and the world system. "They are strangers of the promises of God." They cannot understand our desire to obey the Spirit or the Word of God. Why would they? They know nothing of the plan of God for man or the promises He has given us about our future. They have no hope beyond this world. All the desire and planning they experience has only to do with this life and this world. For them, there is no heaven and life after death, just here and now. This makes them "strangers and foreigners to the things of God and to the hope of God."

What God is telling us about dress is simple; He knows our needs. We are not of this world, and we are not without promise. He has filled our hearts with hope, glorious hope of life eternal. We are in Him and live for Him, and in return, all the hope of heaven is ours now, and His promises of things to come are as sure as if we held them in our hands now. We have set our affection on things above and not on things on earth.

God's Kindgom Inside And Out

In Matthew 6:33, we are told to "Seek first the kingdom of God and His righteousness, and all these things shall be added unto you." The word *seek (zeto)* means to go after; to strive; to pursue; to desire; to aim at; to search for; to endeavor to get. We are to seek to become citizens of God's kingdom and to seek to enroll others in His kingdom, encouraging them to become citizens in God's kingdom.

What is it to be a part of God's kingdom? It means that all of our heart is subjected to God and we have the ability to deny ourselves and take up our cross and follow Him. It isn't going our own way and asking or trusting God to bless what we choose to do. We are to seek to acquire all the perfection of righteousness that was and is in Christ Jesus.

Can we do that now in this body? I think not, at least not to perfection. But we are ever being changed into His image, and one day, when this old flesh is laid aside and we are clothed in righteousness, we shall be like Him, and we shall see Him as He is. The final act of transfiguration will take place when we disrobe from this flesh and are clothed with a new robe of righteousness. We should be living and growing in His grace and knowledge so that there is not so great a change required when He comes. If we apply the verse correctly, we are made seekers, not people who attain. All of life on earth for a believer is spent seeking to know the fullness of God's kingdom. This can only be attained in our life to come in eternity. The fullness of God now is all that He will allow us to experience, and that has much to do with our purpose and intent as seekers. We cannot deceive God, as we often do others and even ourselves. One day after this life is over, we can and shall obtain all that God has in store for us. If God spared not His own Son, how shall He not give us all things?

If the kingdom of God is not sought first, it will never be found. We cannot put God's kingdom on a lower priority than all the other things we seek in this life and expect to find it. If He is not first, something else is, and that will destroy the concept of the Lordship of Christ. He cannot co-reign or reign from any other place in our heart than first place. God is the King in His kingdom. It must be so in our hearts and life. The process involves a dying in us until nothing remains other than His pleasure in us. If we are fully seeking God's kingdom, we are getting rid of all the garbage and things of the world that cannot coexist with the Lord of Glory.

Have you ever cleaned house in anticipation of some guest, perhaps a parent or close friend? You want it all to be clean, comfortable, and in place, showing your commitment to such things and displaying how you want that friend to see you living. How much more should we be willing to labor to remove all the accumulated negatives, believing the King of kings is coming into our life? We would want Him to feel at ease, comfortable, and pleased with all that He sees or hears in our house or life. Think of it from this point of view: as a result of our seeking

Him and seeking Him first, He is willing to condescend to come to where we are and interface with our life, our needs, and our cares and concerns. It would not be wise for us to invite Him into a life of worry and fear, where unbelief and distrust was so vividly displayed.

I remember reading where Jesus went into one house to heal a person who was sick but could not because of the unbelief present in that home. Do we think it is different today? Do we believe He would come into a life that is full of sin and unbelief, where the heart is dark with desire for things of the world, pleasing only the flesh? Saving faith involves the confession of our sins and repenting and turning from those sins and thus inviting Jesus into our lives as Lord and Savior. It appears that many want Him as Savior, which is to be forgiven from their sins, but stop short of asking Him to be their Lord. It is when we are so displeased with how we are living and using our life on earth that we can turn to Him, seeking something better, something other than things to please the flesh, and find in Him a new life and new way to satisfy our soul.

It can be said without hesitation: A person who comes to Christ Jesus confessing his sins and asking for forgiveness and returns immediately to the old way of life, without any sorrow for his sins, did not repent while he was confessing. You can talk about your sins with everyone on earth and never receive power to make a change and turn from those sinful acts. There is only one mediator between God and man, this man, Christ Jesus. There is only one who can forgive our sins and remove the power sin had on us; that is the Lord Jesus Christ.

Paul talked about his conversion often in the Scriptures and says in 2 Corinthians 5:17, "Therefore if any man be in Christ, he is a new creation; old things are passed away; behold all things are become new." There was a death in Paul, a death of all the old things that had held place of honor in his life, but now they were all dead. He said he was a new person after Christ came into his life.

We must not expect any less in our life when we come to Christ. He is moving into us to dwell with us for as long as we live on earth, and He needs and deserves a clean place to live, with an atmosphere that is spiritual and full of peace. We must labor to do all He asks of us in cleaning out the old man's pleasures and installing the new life of Christ. This is the source of great joy and great peace, when we realize how different and good life can be after Christ has moved in. This should be a starting point that leads to continued growth and building a great distance between our new life and the life we are leaving behind. If we had stayed the course, as many have done before us, many of us today would be living above worry and anxiety. It appears to be prevalent today, as many are living for themselves rather than God, not just the unbelievers in the world, but also many who claim to be believers whose manner of dress says something different. I am not suggesting that we are entitled to become judges of our fellow man, but oftentimes the appearance is oblivious.

We have lived in such a way that the world views us as grasshoppers, up and down, ever changing, involved in carnal and fleshly habits one day and singing in church the next day. We have grown so used to moral failure in the church that it is hardly newsworthy anymore. The life of many political leaders has been exposed to appear like something you would see in a porn flick. When it is viewed from a broad point of view, you can see the roots are deep in the idea of living the life of hypocrisy without a deep, abiding faith in God. Giving a place for the Lord to live and a place to rule from will give a man a kind of guard against those vain, ostentatious habits that push us into playing with the flesh and even spending habits that push us beyond a budget and allow for foolish spending. When we learn to share the thought process with the Lord, allowing Him to add His thinking with our own and even allowing us the opportunity to withhold our thoughts until we have heard His own, we can then say we are growing in the grace and knowledge of our Lord and Savior, Jesus Christ. Where is the statement being made by the people of God? Are we to stand by and watch the world go on in its deceitful ways, showing the world what they think is best for us? Can the church not take a stand by letting the world know we are different? Can we not see that what is in our innermost heart is being reflected on the outside? How is it so acceptable today that so few can see the truth about whose we are and how we should reflect His presence and His preference for the way we live? Living by faith to please our Lord should take a higher priority than the desire to please ourselves and/or others.

There should be nothing in us that would think about being dishonest, yet many Christians display the character of a dishonest person. There is a difference between trying to manage our flesh and asking for Him to manage our flesh. If we have the habit of doing what feels right or good and then having to repent for the foolish mistakes, that itself will become a nasty habit. We can learn to surrender each day and moment by moment to His leadership and learn to ask first and seek first to do His wishes in preference to our own, knowing He will not fail us. We can stop the painful cycle of trying to buy or accumulate things that we hope will make us more desirable or appear to be of greater value to the world. We can develop the desire to be more pleasing to Him and of greater value to Him right in our home or on the job. This transformation in the area of our desire is the daily process of seeking first the kingdom of God and His righteousness. The hearts of God's children are part of His kingdom and must prove loyal to our King. The uniform of the church is godliness, with piety and love for one another. We are not to engage in competition to outdress or strive to be more fashionable than someone else. We can determine in our heart and mind that the end of our way on earth will be in pursuit of His kingdom. We may not take every step of every day in that pursuit, but trusting and striving at the same time, much, if not most, of our journey will be toward that goal. There should be no other on earth with a greater desire or determination to reach our goal. Our effort will be as great as any other and more rewarding than all others.

How can we watch the athlete train so long and hard to perfect his sport or the surgeon spend so many long hours to sharpen his skills or any other pursuit of perfection, knowing that the rewards they will reap are like dirt compared to gold for the child of God seeking to be a part of God's kingdom? Can we believe there is no effort required of us? Should we just relax in our normal mode of pleasing the flesh and expect the reward from our Heavenly Father for striving to enter in at the straight gate or seeking first His kingdom? *The reward is not in the labor; the labor is the result of our trusting.*

Faith will produce the effort needed to make the transformation by His Spirit possible. When James said, "Faith without works is dead," he was not saying the result of works is faith but that the result of having a living faith in God will produce works (James 2:17). One part of that faith-produced work is seeking God's kingdom as priority one. It is the excellence of what we pursue and the glory it brings to the One for whom we extend our effort that makes it all worthwhile. We are benefited by it all, but our benefit should not enter the picture of our mind until we are well on our way.

It would appear today that many, if not most, of the Christians in this nation are a bit lazy or at least uninterested in a hot pursuit of the things of God. Listen to some of the men at church talking about their golf game or fishing, catch the tone of excitement and zeal in their voice, and try to find its equal in discussing evangelism or seasons of prayer.

During the years of my pastorate, I felt burdened by God to provide opportunity for seasons of prayer for the church, for the lost in the community, for our outreach and mission program, and for the sick in our congregation. When those times of prayer began, it was like trying to keep delinquent children in the schoolroom. It wasn't uncommon to find small groups standing in the hallway swapping stories or telling jokes. Some were there with broken hearts and in earnest prayer, seeking God's directions and answers to our prayers, but the others seemed more interested in dampening the spirit and purpose for our being there.

Here is what I learned from those times: I learned to be patient in my pursuit but ever so persistent. I was made aware of the heart of God on the subject and realized that what others failed to do did not erase what I was wanting to experience. I learned that there would be opposition to all I desired to accomplish for God, and Satan himself would see to it. I even learned to recognize the ones he would use to try to disrupt God's plan and God's program. They had failed to see the work as belonging to the Father and therein failed to realize they were opposing God, not me. The Bible warns that we and all who live righteously in Christ Jesus would suffer persecution. I took it as confirmation that the desire to enhance God's church by these seasons of prayer was indeed given to me by the Lord, and my work was done in the organization of the meetings.

When we are earnestly seeking God's kingdom and His righteousness, we should expect opposition. Learn to find encouragement in this and not discouragement. The Lord is pleased to give us all we need to endure the offense and bring us to a place of strength and a place of peace. If we did not have those times of trial and opposition, we could not appreciate the hours of peace and love. If we did not have times of sickness and pain, we could not appreciate being healthy. Times of sadness will make you laugh when joy comes, and it will always come. We may have to wait for morning, as we read in Psalm 30:5: "…weeping may endure for the night, but joy cometh in the morning." Isaiah gave a great promise from the Lord in 40:31: "But they that wait upon the Lord shall renew their strength; they shall mount up on wings like eagles; they shall run, and not be weary; and they shall walk, and not faint."

Do not despair, and do not give up or quit. Stay the course; you are not alone, and the One with you is greater than the one that is in the world. Be quiet in your spirit and listen to what He says and watch what He will show you as He leads you to better things. All the negative is nothing more than persecution intended to discourage you and hopefully cause you to stop in your pursuit. Don't do it! Stay on course and be patient; even when you fail, God will not turn His back on you. His ears and eyes are open to any sign you may give asking for His intervention. He will surely give the victory because He is always victorious and His victory is our victory also.

Pray daily and often that He would make it His desire and the desire of His Son and the Holy Spirit to assist you in making Him and His kingdom first place in your life. Let the things go and other things die that need to be removed, and allow Him to replace them with what He knows you need. He will do it! Keep in mind the flower that is so beautiful in His sight, and this beauty is all that is asked of the lily. Being beautiful involves only giving our consent and our yielding to His will. That flower must grow from seed to stem and from stem to leaf and stronger still stem before it ever bursts forth in bloom. God alone can see the bloom in the seed. He knows what is coming forth because He designed it and He alone desired it, and He alone awaits its beauty.

So it is with every one of God's children. When we first came to Him, we were like the seed, but He could see the full bloom.

As the seed needs rain and sun, God alone could give as needed in the right amount and the right kind of food for growth. God alone can give us what we need to grow strong and beautiful for His kingdom pleasure. The difficult times are allowed so that we might develop strength for service. During the long, dark night, the plant reaches up toward the light until morning brings just what is needed, and then, only then, will the bloom appear. Our nights may seem long and lonely and, at times, be filled with pain and sorrow. Sleep may escape our weak bodies, but just as sure as night came, so will come the sunrise and, with the sun, all that is needed to drive away the loneliness and pain and cause praise to replace them.

What did the bird find? He found that God in His goodness has placed in him the directions and desire to go to the place of feeding and the place of rest. Without fail, God continues to this day to provide all they need for food and shelter. What did man find as to his stature or longevity? He found that he cannot add one cubit to his size or one hour to his lifespan because God had already predetermined both and made it part of His great plan. What did the lily find? It found that it was more beautiful in God's eyes than Solomon in all his kingly apparel. We can find in our pursuit of life a providence that will allow us to do all we do in response to God's purpose and desire for us, allowing us to seek Him and His kingdom first along with His righteousness, making us ready for and able to enjoy eternity as part of the great kingdom of God.

Ascending Faith

As a result of seeking God's kingdom and His righteousness first, "all these things shall be added unto you." "All these things" refers to food, shelter, all that is needed for life, and clothing for our body. The word *added* can be substituted with the word *given* but with caution. It is best interpreted as "be made available" to you. God gives opportunities much more than He does items. If I needed $10 for something that was honorable in God's sight, I would not ask that I would find it walking down the street, nor would I hope to find it growing on a tree outside my window. I know that nothing is impossible with God, but that does not fairly represent how God thinks. To be honest with you on this subject, if I needed $10 and had only $9, I would probably give the $9 away and trust God for the $10. It would make no difference with God as to the amount needed, only the amount and quality of faith that brought the need to His attention.

I do not mean that in the context of seedtime and harvest. That idea has been used and abused so much by some of the TV brothers that it is embarrassing for me to even think about it. Nothing will motivate God to move on your behalf except faith. If you do not have faith in God and you have needs that you cannot address, I suggest you find someone who does have the right kind of faith and hope so that you can persuade them to seek God's help on your behalf.

My mother, who is a woman of great faith, has spent most of her life praying for others. I have watched her working in the home while I was yet a very young lad. All the while she worked she was praying. Sometimes while singing a song, she would end a verse of the song with words of a prayer already on her heart. She prayed for people she did not know, but somehow, God had placed on her heart the need to pray for these people. I have gone with Mom in the late hours of the night when she was summoned to assist someone in need and only Mother's prayers would meet the need. I grew up admiring her ability to pray so much and for so many people, many of them she would never meet face to face in this life.

On one occasion, I was traveling from North Carolina to Virginia to introduce a friend to some key people in a business I knew. He needed help in getting to know these people in order to help his business. I listened for several hours to his explanations about all the things wrong in his life and the great need he felt in his heart. I told him about Mom's prayer life and suggested she would be a great influence on him. Without his knowing the route I was taking, we were less than a mile from Mom's house about the time he said, "I would sure like to meet your mother."

I said, "That is good news because we are just a few blocks from her house." I had taken a route through east Tennessee, knowing we could stop just long enough to check on Mom. He could hardly speak at all.

When we entered Mom's house, I introduced her to my friend and told her he needed her prayers. I wish all could have seen and heard how Mom dealt with the situation. She told us she knew we were coming and had just taken her apron off and walked to the door. She said she saw my car coming down the street and was pleased to know her anticipation was confirmed. Without asking anything about my friend's problems, Mom walked a few steps to her favorite chair in the living room and knelt on her knees. She began to pray but stopped suddenly and motioned for my friend and myself to join her on our knees. Not a word had been spoken about this man's troubles, but yet Mother listed every one of them just as he had shared them with me. In fact, I think she has listed them in the same order he had shared them with me. When the prayer had ended, we both walked out to the car; my friend did not say a word.

I drove for several miles and was back on the highway to Virginia when all of a sudden my friend shouted, "Stop the car. Stop the car." I pulled into a vacant driveway to some business that had closed up.

He began weeping loudly and said, "I can't go any farther. I am lost. I need the Lord in my life. All the while your mother was praying for me, I felt like my insides were on fire. It was as if hot oil was running down from my head and all over my body. I was so afraid I could not speak. Just now, it has become clear to me. The reason for my problems is that I might see my need for God. Show me how to be saved. Show me how to pray like your mother prayed."

I led the man to Christ, had prayer with him, and continued on toward our destination. Mother had prayed that this man would learn to trust Christ as his Lord and Savior, that God would help him with his many problems, and that God would bless our efforts that day in meeting what we hoped would be a new customer. We had not been in the place of business in Virginia more than twenty minutes when a contract was signed and the man gained the largest customer he had for his business. He could not stop singing the praise of Mother's prayers, but I reassured him time and again, "It is all a matter of the quality of our faith in the Master."

Let me be clear about this matter of "quality of faith." If you have known sin in your life and are doing nothing about it, your prayer life is hindered, and the quality of your faith at that moment is less than effective. Sin, all sin, is a barrier between God and His children. I hear it so often: "But God knows my heart." Yes, He does, and He knows the truth about your heart and motives. An attempt to justify your sin will certainly limit your ability to trust God. We must know the origin of our faith is God and not ourselves. God has given to us the measure of faith, allowing us to believe on Him and obey His word. Faith cannot be created or made strong within us apart from His work through the Holy Spirit. We can allow Him, by simple trust, to do the work of faith within us, resulting in the level or measure of faith we possess.

The Master told a few in the New Testament they had "great faith" and "so great a faith." These were people who had divested themselves from the world and focused their hope and affection on the Lord Jesus alone, not the admixture we see in so many lives today. We seem to think we can mix our faith in Christ Jesus with a little sin, a little wrong behavior, and maybe a little dishonesty, and still expect answers to our prayers and a sweet fellowship with God. James tells us the double-minded man should not expect to receive anything from God. He also points out that this man is unstable in all his ways. This problem seems to be growing larger and worse as time goes by, and the negative effect it is having on the Christians and the church is alarming.

There is, in my opinion, an apathy, a worldliness that is hurting the cause of Christ and turning His church into places of entertainment and/or the place to go for good political debate. I feel in my heart a desire to cry out as loud as I can, *"Let the church be His church. Get the world out of His church and sin out of the hearts of His people, and allow us all to focus on Him and His great love."*

With the weakness in so many hearts today, it is clear as to why there is so much worry and anxiety. The need for His presence and power in our lives has never been greater, and yet with all the pieces of the world's system mixed in with our faith, we are anemic and powerless. There is more injustice and more visible sin in our nation today than I ever remember seeing or hearing about, and yet the church of Jesus Christ is more quiet and out of sight than I ever remember.

At the time of this writing, I am living in California and hear over and over again that this is a gray state. It is as if someone wants me to apologize for being black and white. I am not in the habit of watering down everything that is precious to me or hiding my convictions and Christian beliefs under the rug so no one will think I am a Christian, a believer of God's Word, the Bible. The desire of my heart is not to be gray nor even appear to be gray; I am a Christian. I have no desire to hold any of this world in my heart. I feel the need to be as close to my Lord Jesus as I possibly can. I know that involves me cleaning my heart and mind from as much of this world as I can, with His help, which is my daily conquest. Nothing will move us closer to Him than evicting all sin and the world from our heart and asking the Holy Spirit of God to fill every open place in us with His presence and power. Then we must pray He will use us, all of us, for His purpose and empower us to war against the world, its evil, and the devil.

This is a war, and we are all soldiers in the army of God. Do not be a coward or a deserter. God help us to take a stand and be joyfully counted among the righteous for His glory and our good.

Without faith, the kind of faith that will allow us to acknowledge the presence and power of the Lord Jesus with us, we cannot face the demands of this life or this world and remain true to our convictions. Faith should be an understood fact in our life. That is, we should understand the limits of our faith or the strength of our faith. We can know the value of faith if we gain the understanding before the storms come and the demands of life become so strong. It is different with each believer and must be tested in order for us to know where we stand in our faith.

Allow me to share a few examples with you from God's Word. In Mark 4:40, it says, "And Jesus said unto them, why are you so fearful? How is it that you have no faith?" Christ is talking to His disciples while in a boat that is experiencing a storm. Jesus had been sleeping during the wind, lightning, and thunder sounding. It wasn't the noise of the storm that had awakened our Lord but the sound of His disciples' voices, crying out in fear, "Master, carest thou not that we perish?" (verse 38). Following Christ will not provide a life without fear for us. These men were His closest friends and were with Him every day, but here they were in a storm and crying out for fear.

Christ allowed the storm to strike the boat and allowed the wind and lightning to arouse the fear in His disciples' hearts, but He did not allow the storm to sink the boat. Rightly understood, these men would not be in the situation facing them if they were not serving the Lord Jesus. The Master teacher was at work here and wanting His disciples to embrace the ascending faith that reminds them that when a crisis comes, we are to look for the Savior, not at the situation. The mighty God of creation was with them in the boat, and they did not see Him. He wanted to deepen their faith by taking them though the storm, not around it. Had they paid attention to the Master's words, they could have avoided the fear and crying out.

In verse thirty-five, the Lord had said to them, "Let us pass over unto the other side." That sounds to me like He had a destination in mind. He knew the ending of the matter before the beginning. They could not see at that time what He saw. Neither can we. No one can see into the tomorrows of their life, but He can. What we can do is trust Him with unlimited trust; that will allow us to weather the storms of life, believing He will take us through. I am thankful we cannot see the coming storms, thankful that we are required to have faith in Him in order to survive.

Peter writes in 1 Peter 4:12, "Beloved, think it not strange concerning the fiery trial which is to test you, as though some strange thing happened unto you." We should all know that between here and the safe landings in our lives there are the storms. When the storms come, and they will certainly come, I want to be in the boat where Jesus is. We can know the victories He is providing if we can be where He is and know it.

Jesus rebuked them concerning their faith, saying they had "no faith." Jesus, when awakened, rebuked the sea. He did not change the ship they were in; He changed the sea. God's way of looking at every situation of life is different than man's point of view. The faith we need to embrace says the Lord is in charge, in charge of all the issues of our life, and we can and should trust Him completely.

I have been on the Galilee and have seen how suddenly these storms can arise. Our lives are like that, calm one minute and in the midst of a storm the next. We need an abiding faith that cannot be caught off guard. When we face the storms without understanding and without faith, we will always experience fear. When we face the storms of life in faith and can believe the Master is there with us, we will experience His calm. What an insult to any believer to be told by our Lord Jesus that we have no faith. Sometimes it feels like our faith may be so very small, but no faith?

Another passage of Scripture that deals with the measure of our faith is Matthew 16:8: "Which, when Jesus perceived, he said unto them, O ye of little faith, why reason you among yourselves, because ye have brought no bread?" Of course, the passage is dealing with the feeding of the four thousand men, plus the women and children. There is usually some effort to imagine how many people were fed in total count. It really isn't important to the moral of the story at all.

The character assigned to the faith of the disciples on this occasion is "little faith." I fear that many of the people in the church pews today would identify with this term. Little faith in this story has to do with the lack of understanding. The disciples had little faith to understand what the Master was doing or teaching.

How good it would be if we could, by faith, come to understand what He wants to do in our life, to see His goal and understand why we must face some of the things in life that come our way and not lose sight of His leading all the way. No matter how demanding the task before us, we must trust the fact of His presence with us. Trouble comes and we don't understand, but we know He is there with us and is working it all together for our good and His glory.

Apparently the disciples did not understand this and felt some intimidation about their inability to feed those present on that day. The Master wanted them to see His ability, without question, to provide all that was needed. He blessed the seven loaves and the few fish and multiplied it to an amount so large that all were fed and seven baskets full of broken pieces were gathered up after the meal. I believe He could have created the loaves and fish had there not been any present for Him to bless. If the same situation were before us today, it would be the equivalent of the Lord blessing one Happy Meal and feeding a hundred thousand at a NASCAR event. Bottom line: nothing is impossible with God. Until we are able to embrace that fact, we will struggle using "little faith" in dealing with all of our problems and uncertainties.

In Matthew 15:28 Jesus teaches about one with "great" faith. What an honor for God to view your faith as "great faith". I suppose this to be one of the greatest compliments ever given to a human. "Then Jesus answered and said unto her, O woman, great is thy faith; be it unto thee even as thou wilt. And her daughter was made well from that very hour." This, of course, is the story of the Syrophenician woman, also found in the gospel of Mark 7:24-30. This lady followed Jesus one day, crying out and begging for His mercy on her daughter, who was possessed with a demon spirit. One might conclude after reading these verses that Jesus has been rude or harsh with this lady, but on careful examination, we can learn that His words to her were His way of helping her to believe in Him as the Son of God. When she addressed the Lord, she called Him the Son of David, but after the exchange of words, she calls Him, "Lord." We should note in the beginning of the story, Jesus had left the area where His ministry had been determined, but knowing of this lady's need, He took another way into the Gentile area of Tyre and Sidon. In verse twenty-five, she is seen worshipping Jesus, indicating that the goal of the Master is met.

The cry of this lady is not different from the cry of many parents today. She saw that her daughter was under the influence of Satan (a demon). Although today it is viewed somewhat differently, the influence is the same. It appears as if the disciples had concluded by the Lord's ignoring the lady for some time that He was not interested in helping a Gentile. The truth is He knew the lady would be there and knew she had the need she expressed to the Savior. No doubt He wanted some rest and peace for Himself and the disciples, and the only way He could find such a place would be away from the Jewish territory. However, it was always His custom to make every minute count, and He used this diversion from the daily routine to reach another soul and teach another great lesson.

When the Master responded to the lady's request, He told her, "O woman, great is thy faith..." Now I admit, I would love to hear the Lord say that my faith is great, but I am not sure we can know just how the Lord appraises our faith. What I want you to see today is the fact that in God's eyes, there are multiple levels of faith. Even in the lives of believers, there are different levels of faith.

In Matthew's gospel, chapter eight and verse ten, we read, "When Jesus heard it he marveled and said to them that followed, 'Verily I say unto you, I have not found so great faith, no, not in Israel.'" Here is another level of faith expressed by the Master; it is "so great faith." The story is that of Jesus healing a centurion's servant. Jesus was teaching in Capernaum when the Centurion came to Him, and his servant was lying at home, grievously tormented. The Lord replied that he would go with him to meet with the servant, no doubt with the intent to heal him. The Centurion, however, told Jesus that he was not worthy for Him to enter into his home but asked if He would just say the words and his servant would be healed. He then drew a comparison between his authority and the authority of the Lord Jesus. It was in response to this comparison that Jesus made the assessment of the man's faith.

The purpose in the Master's heart is to prove His power in receiving all who truly believe Him and power to reject any who do not, even the religious crowd. This is in evidence to the fact that He is the Messiah from Israel. The Centurion was a Gentile, and Jesus was a Jew; there was no public association between the two, and yet Jesus was willing to reply to the request of this Gentile because of his faith in the Master's power to meet his need.

I believe it was the humility of the Centurion that gained the attention of the Lord Jesus. The man did not ask for himself but for another, and he asked in passion with a full heart of belief. All of his hope was focused on Jesus alone. Even though he did not feel worthy for the Master to enter his house, he believed the compassion of the Lord was such that He would hear his request.

Look at His reply to the man's request: "I will." It was not only His determination but also His readiness to overcome the racial differences, the social barriers, and any other differences between the two of them and meet the need. Luke wrote in (Acts 10:34-35,) "There is no respect of persons with God, but in every nation he that feareth him, and worketh righteousness, is accepted with him." This man was able to take his focus off of himself and look completely to Jesus for help. He did not come deserving or demanding anything from the Lord. He only came in humility, realizing he could do nothing but the One before him could do all that was needed and more.

Just the opposite was true in the Lord's reply. He focused only on His power to meet the man's request and knew that He was God, with unlimited power to apply to any man who asks with unlimited faith. Here again, we see the quick and powerful response from God when we come to Him with more than fundamental faith, more than weak religious routine, but in the ascending faith that lets us know He, the God of the universe and heaven, is there with us at the time of need. Oh, that we could learn not to fear the situations that bring us to our knees but learn to see at those special and precious moments that He is there with us in mind and us on His heart. How different it will be when our faith rises to the level of moving the heart of God in response to our cry for help.

My next thought on faith is from Acts 6:5: "And the saying pleased the whole multitude; and they chose Stephen, a man full of faith and of the Holy Spirit, and Phillip, and Prochorus, and…" Notice the term "full of faith." The passage is about the beginning of deacons, a new concept for the church and a new ministry for the church. The need that was being addressed was a lack of attention to the daily needs of the church family. One of the problems was the neglect of the widows. The grumbling, complaining, and constant criticisms were causing division among the membership and had grown to be a distraction to the purpose of the church. The disciples agreed it was not wise for them to leave the ministry of the Word in order to attend to all the lesser matters that were rising daily in the church. So they set the standard and chose men who possessed those standards and ordained them to attend those problems, allowing the apostles to attend to the more weighty matters of preaching, praying, and making disciples.

Stephen was assessed to be full of faith and was ordained for the new office.

If a glass of water lacks one drop in order to be full, we cannot accurately say the glass is full of water. Add the one drop lacking and then declare the glass full of water. If we have a strange admixture of our desires and the Lord's desires in our heart, we cannot say we are full of His desires. By the way, any admixture of God and any part of the world, including ourselves, will rule out the Lordship of Christ Jesus in our lives. Remember the old saying, "He is Lord of all or not Lord at all?" To be full of faith is to be emptied of all else. No other demand on our spiritual loyalty. Our worship is shared with nothing and no one else. Our focus is on the Lord and His word. All that He says we will do, and whatever we must bear in order to be proven true to His name and His cause, we will do. Still, this will not equal being full of faith.

In order to claim this level of faith, we must rule out all doubt and hesitation. It would require us to be constantly ready to respond to His will without any delay and without any doubt. How I wish for all believers to be full of faith. It is, however, a goal to work toward without ever arriving. If we were full of faith today, we should desire and work toward being full of faith tomorrow. The demands of each day are different than the days before and may well require a difference in the application of faith. We can only continue in the fullness of faith by the daily walk with the Master, "trusting as the days go by, trusting as the moment fly, trusting what ever befalls, trusting Jesus, that is all."

The idea is a continual walking with Him and a continual staying in touch with Him to know His leading. The danger is for us to assume we know what He wants us to do without ever asking, never taking time to commune with Him in such a way that we know His directions for His church and our lives. The word *continually* (*proskarteresomen*) is to continue steadfastly; to persevere; to continue on and on, sticking to it. We are to never let up or back off, always seeking Him. It often appears that some are seeking a religious experience instead of seeking Him. When a situation arises that brings us to our knees, we often stay just long enough to voice our request and claim the answer in Jesus's name; amen. The idea is to see Him, not His response to our needs. The key to fullness of faith is learning to abide in His presence day after day, year after year, until we are so sensitive to His voice, His Spirit, that our hearts are brighter and full of joy just because He is with us as He said He would be.

Another reference to faith is found in Romans 4:19: "And being not weak in faith, he considered not his own body now dead, when he was about a hundred years old, neither yet the deadness of Sarah's womb." The whole of this passage is dealing with faith and justification. There is no justification without faith. Abraham believed God to the most extreme measure. He believed God could make alive those who were dead and call things into existence where they were not. He found in God a hope when there was no hope, even in numbers great enough to make a great nation of people that did not exist. Because of this faith, he believed God would allow him to be physically strong enough to do what other men his age could not do. At the age of one hundred years, with no strength left in the physical man and a wife who was many years past the age of childbearing, Abraham believed God would give him a son, through which the nation of

Israel would be born. He believed God was fully able to do all that He had promised, and God accounted this to him as righteousness. Simply put, God counted Abraham's strong faith as evidence of trusting Him for whatever could come into his life.

Think about it for a moment: Abraham was asked to believe the impossible but declared by faith that nothing is impossible with God. The source of Abraham's faith is God. The source of our faith is God. Faith is not something we can muster up in our hearts and put to work. Faith is God's gift to us, and we are to learn to use it in such a way as to allow it to grow strong and eventually become first place in our life. When our faith is strong, God is first in our life, and when God is first in our life, we can exercise the faith He has given us so that it grows stronger and stronger. There was nothing in Abraham that allowed God to use him but faith. It was not faith added to an already successful life; it was faith alone.

Abraham could not have imagined having a son, and by Sarah. He was one hundred, and she was near the same age. Abraham must have reasoned God to be the Omnipotent God, who can make something out of nothing. Have you ever considered the promises of God as being promises that only He can fulfill? No one has ever been able to provide what God has promised to provide. No one has ever been needed to fulfill God's promises because God always does what He says He will do.

Think how strong the relationship between God and Abraham must have been to produce such faith. I am sure the relationship is not restricted to just one man. If fact, I believe we could all have such relationship with God if we allowed ourselves to believe God as Abraham did.

We must be teaching ourselves to doubt instead of believe. I fear too that we are teaching our children to doubt instead of believing God. Even when God gave Abraham the promise, he did not stagger; that is, he did not waver. The word *stag-*

ger (*diakrino*) means he did not vacillate; he did not question God. He was fully convinced that God was able to do all that He said He would do. With many of us, and much of the time, we believe God *can* do what He says He will do, but we do not believe He *will* do all that He said He would do.

The difference is results. Abraham was not weak in faith, and God accepts it as being strong. Where are we on the subject? Is our faith weak, and does it need to be made strong? It will require exercise, and the more we use faith, the stronger it will grow. Perhaps we could be as strong in faith as Abraham was. It is a matter of our willingness to trust God and learn to live each day by faith and not by carnal routine. Realize all that God has made available to us through faith. The only thing we have as believers that is better than faith is love.

Faith is not a timid matter but one of great power and force. Coupled with love, what on earth could overpower God's servant when we have this mighty shield of faith? Without an ascending faith that is growing each day as we face the assault from the world and all that is sinful, we will be at mercy of the world. It doesn't take much to trip some of us up, but it is all a matter of faith.

I believe the tears that are wiped away from the eyes of the believers by Christ Himself, just as we enter into heaven, are tears of sorrow when we realize what we could have done for Him and the kingdom if only we had exercised our faith, allowing it to grow into a useful tool. "…According to your faith be it unto you" (Matthew 9:29). We have as much of Jesus as we believe we can have, and we receive from God in the same measure, according to our faith. Many receive little because they believe little, even when they have asked for much.

After cursing the fig tree in Matthew 21, Jesus began to teach His disciples about faith. In verses twenty-one through twenty-two, it says:

> Jesus answered and said unto them, "Verily I say unto you, if ye have faith, and doubt not, ye shall not only do this which is done to the fig tree, but also if ye shall say unto this mountain, be thou removed, and be thou cast into the sea, it shall be done. And all things, whatever ye shall ask in prayer, believing, ye shall receive."

Christ Jesus has just displayed His power over nature again and is using the occasion to teach His disciples about the power of faith. The lesson is rather simple and one would think easy to learn, but that isn't the case. Christ has promised to give us all things whatever we ask in prayer. This is in response to our believing on Him without any doubt.

Have you had a prayer recently that wasn't answered? Could the reason we pray so little be linked to the fact that so few of our prayers are answered? If we really believed all our prayers would be answered, how could anyone ever get us away from the prayer closet? The most sought-after person in the world would be the Christian who knows how to pray without doubt. The top of every recruiter's list would be "one who knows how to pray without doubt." Jesus told Peter in Luke 22:32 that He had prayed for him "that his faith fail not." I sure hope the Master has prayed thus for me and for you. What could be more discouraging than a failing faith?

Keeping with our main thought, living above worry, we can see the parallel between faith and worry. The stronger our faith, the less we will worry. The lesser or weaker our faith, the more we will worry and deal with anxiety. I think it is fair to assume that the progression of our faith is pleasing to God and expresses our trust in Him, as He has prescribed. The opposite is also true; the weaker our faith, the more prone we are to distrust Him and cause Him shame and disappointment by allowing others to see and/or know about our worry and anxiety. This will surely say to the world around us that we do not trust the Lord as we should nor as His Word invites us to trust.

I remember as a young boy how my mother would check to see if my ears and my fingernails were clean before she would let me go to school or church or anywhere in public. She was concerned that someone might think she was not a good mother if they saw me unclean. I don't remember wearing many new clothes, and I was never concerned with what was fashionable or the new styles or fads, but I do remember being told over and over again that I would be clean. So it was with all the family; we were never to go into public without Mom's inspection. I don't know if it was true with other children, but our mom would ask about our underwear to be sure we were not wearing something that was not clean and without any tear or unmended spot. I thought for the longest time that clean and untorn underwear would keep me from accidents or ever needing to go to the hospital. What Mom was saying makes a lot of good sense now. She was concerned as to how people would view her and Dad if they saw me less than clean and properly dressed. How I presented myself to the public reflected on her and Dad.

Is this not true with our Heavenly Father? Does our little faith not say to the world that our Father is slacking or lacking in areas of faith? Can He not provide for His own, or can He not protect His children? When we display our worry and anxiety for the world to see, is there not someone who is thinking, *I thought the Christian life was protected from those things of the world?* It is when the world sees us go through the storms of life without falling apart, when we bury a loved one without giving up all hope, or watch a life of work and savings go down with a major medical bill or the house go up in smoke that they are made to realize the children of God do have something worthwhile.

More than anything else, I do not want the Lord Jesus to ever hesitate in displaying me as His servant or prevent anyone from seeing me or knowing me as His servant. Please understand, I am not perfect, not by a long shot, but my heart belongs to Him, and my faith, which is still growing, is far, far greater than it was but not yet as great as I hope to see it grow into. We are always a work in progress, until He calls us home. We must continue to grow stronger in faith and deeper in devotion until we leave this world. Our faith in God is the only thing that will help us to grow in His image.

I have so many times isolated all the verses of Scripture that deal with the believer's faith and read them over and over again, all the while praying that I could learn something that would result in my faith growing stronger and my life resembling His life more. It was in these pursuits that I learned just how alive God's Word is and how strong it is in turning our life from one way to another. Coupled with prayer, faith can and will move the mountains in our lives and uproot the trees of doubt that need to be cast far away from us. It is the topic of prayer that I want to focus our attention on for a while and help you understand how prayer plays a big role in the process of learning to live above worry and anxiety.

Your level of faith depends on your investment in prayer. A person who has a strong faith is always strong in prayer. A lack of faith will hinder or stop the praying process. James said, "You have not because you ask not" (James 4:2). The fact of the matter is you will not ask unless you have faith enough to believe He will answer your prayer. Sometimes prayer is offered out of desperation but does not have any faith. It is merely a religious routine, with nothing more than a carnal hope that God may pity the person and do something in response to their calling on His name. The call is not the issue; it is the call of faith that demands a response. Like any loving Father, He enjoys knowing

His children can come to Him with any request, and nothing is too large or too costly for Him to hesitate in giving an answer.

A friend in Jordan was telling me of the counsel his father had given him on this subject of faith. He said he had been taught to envision a large room in heaven that contained all the answers to all of his prayers for a lifetime then to think about going to heaven after death and learn the room is still full because he had not trusted God enough to ask for the gifts stored in that room. It will be awesome if we never received His gifts of love because we never asked Him. It is lack of faith that prevents us from asking the Father. It is ascending faith that embraces His presence and trusts His heart for the reply we need. A fundamental faith says we should pray. An ascending faith says He is there with us when we pray. He knows our need and loves us so much that He cannot refuse to honor our faith. If we love Him and trust Him thus, we will be prompted by His Holy Spirit to ask for those things He is willing to give and do for us. If we do not exhibit a love for Him and a trust in Him, why should He give us the desires of our heart?

Prayer is Essential

Our Lord Jesus teaches on the subject of prayer in Matthew 6. It is here we will take our thoughts for the effort of learning to live above worry and anxiety by the use of ascending faith expressed in our prayers. Jesus begins in verses five and six by warning about the wrong motive and the right motive for praying. I hope you will see how contemporary His teaching is. Reading these verses again reads like something in the daily newspaper.

And when thou prayest, thou shalt not be as the hypocrites are; for they love to pray standing in the synagogues and in the corners of the streets, that they may be seen of men. Verily I say unto you, They have their reward. But thou when thou prayest, enter into thy closet, and when thou has shut the door, pray to thy Father, which is in secret; and thy Father which seeth in secret shall reward thee openly.

Matthew 6:5-6 (KJV)

I know of no greater act in the life of a believer than prayer. Nowhere in Scripture does the Lord say, "*if* you pray," but again and again He said, "But *when* you pray." He assumes that those who are truly born again by the Spirit of God will pray. God is the source of all we need and should be the source of all we desire to receive. If we believe that, we will see the need to pray.

Prayer without faith is a foolish waste of words and time. To invest time in prayer, when done in the fashion our Lord teaches us, will prove to be life's greatest investment. Christ draws our attention to the wrong reason to pray: "to be seen of men." He adds, "They have their reward." That is to say, they, having been seen of men, have received all they can get from such an exercise. The purpose of this is to be seen in the eyes of men as being holy or spiritual. Of course, we know there is more to living a holy life than saying words in public. However, there are those who will see the esteem of men as great treasure and will do almost anything to gain such esteem. I, for one, cannot understand why anyone would choose the approval of man in preference to the approval of God. The man who is born again will pray not to be heard by men but to be heard by God. I have often wondered what was in the heart and mind of some of the people I have heard praying. Everything from sermons to weather reports or complete political agendas have been given. I was standing next to a pastor in his church as the offering was to be received. He called on one of his deacons to pray for the offering that day. The deacon began his prayer, but the pastor would whisper the words before the man prayed them. The deacon always prayed the same prayer every time he was called on to pray. The point to be noted is the difference in saying a prayer and praying a prayer. We must never assume that quoting a prayer from memory is equal to praying a prayer from the heart. Every believer will pray, and those who utilize their faith toward its full potential will pray often. There may be long seasons of prayer, and there may be continual praying in a mental awareness of being in God's divine presence. It is prayer that God chose as a means of communication with man as well as communion with man. Without prayer, there is neither communication nor communion with God in a person's life.

God desires to fellowship with man. I think this might be the most misunderstood fact in all of creation. Perhaps because we hold such a high view of God, we think, *What on earth could He desire from me?* We may forget that it was God's love for us that resulted in our salvation. It is His love that motivates Him to want to commune with us and to interface daily with us. When we fail to realize how much God cares about each of us, we will fail to bring our hearts, full of praise, into His presence through prayer. Without prayer, we cannot be aware of being in His presence, and the joy of communion and fellowship will not be experienced.

Living the Christian life is living daily, moment by moment, in full awareness that we are always before the Lord. We may forget from time to time, depending on how intense our relationship with Him is. We may be distracted by other things in our lives, depending on the priority structure of our life. But we will never be able to take one breath without His being there with us, in us, and for us. It is when we realize this vital truth about His love for us and His presence with us that we move from an everyday, fundamental faith into an ascending faith that is always reaching upward, ever closer to Him. In the fullness of His presence is all we are looking for or could ever hope to obtain or achieve. This is living above worry.

Don't deceive yourself about effective praying; it is hard work, but it works. The one most important key to spiritual growth is a successful prayer life. Leave it out of your daily diet and you become weak, anemic, and ineffective in sharing your faith with another person and ineffective in finding real joy and purpose in your walk with God. You just cannot get from where you are to where you want to be in service to Christ Jesus without prayer.

Prayer is a result of knowing God, but prayer does not mean a person truly knows the Lord.

There may be some measure of psychological relief experienced by the exercise of prayer, especially if it is done on a regular basis. This relief does not mean God had anything to do with the prayer or the person doing the praying. It is merely a physical process and a physical response. When God hears and answers our prayers, it is the release of heaven's power to meet our need. There is no substitute for God's answer and no way the world or the devil can give the peace and joy we experience when we know, without a doubt, our God has responded to our request.

The measure of time you spend in praying in public versus the time you spend praying in private may well indicate what your purpose in prayer really is. The world can stop us from doing many things, but there is no way anyone or anything can stop us from praying. If we love the Lord and love time with Him, we can engage and enjoy being with Him anytime and anywhere. In all of life's travels and all of life's experiences, I have never seen the moment that I could not pray. Most of the times we pray in public, we will either be standing or sitting at a table, but the best time I have invested in prayer was time when I bowed on my knees at a place set aside for prayer and was not rushed by time nor interrupted by any other sound and just talked with the Master.

I was taught as a child that I needed to choose a place and set a time to meet with the Lord every day of my life. I have made that appointment and tried very hard to keep it, and most of the time I have succeeded, but it seemed that the time allotted was not enough and had to be increased. The other things in life that some seem to be addicted to, things of entertainment or pleasure, I just can't get interested in. Oftentimes while watching something on TV that I thought would be of interest to me, I felt the need to go apart and talk with my Master. Never have I been disappointed with what He brought to those meetings. He may have been disappointed in me, but He always showed up with just what I needed.

My wife and I spent a number of years in a small, rural community, where we farmed several acres of land and tended to several head of cattle. Oftentimes during those days, I would talk with the Lord while plowing with the tractor or working in the fields. Sometimes late at night, trying to finish the day's work, I could feel my heart crying out within me to be alone with Jesus. It was so easy, with no distractions around, to just talk with Him—no one around for miles, no traffic or cell phones, no TV or radio, just the night, my Lord, and me. I could speak as loud as I wanted to, knowing no one could hear me. I could relate so many experiences from those times of prayer, but I want to stay focused on prayer and the faith required for effective praying.

Those meetings with God were secret meetings for me. God sees in secret and answers in secret. Many may know later about it, but the experience is between you and God. Two may be praying side by side, but each are having a secret meeting with God. That is why the scheduled meeting time and place is so important, a time and a place that is reserved only for you and the Lord Jesus. He may answer you openly if He chooses to do so, but He remains in secret. He is not interested in display. He is not interested in gaining the approval of the crowds. He is only interested in meeting one-on-one and sharing His heart with your heart. If it isn't personal, God isn't there.

Why is it so difficult for believers to keep daily appointments with God? In light of who He is and what His desire is for us, why should we not be able to keep our appointments? What else is there on earth that could tempt us to be drawn away from Him? There is nothing more satisfying, more needed for the child of God, than to be in communion and fellowship with Him. I don't know if there is such a thing as too much time with Him.

I know we need to be busy about the Father's business, and that means sharing our faith with those around us in the world. You will not share your faith effectively, and probably not at all, if you do not spend an adequate amount of time in prayer with the Father. When we desire others to know our Lord Jesus, we should begin in prayer, seeking His directions and blessings in reaching that loved one. What we have to share with them is the result of our time in prayer and fellowship with the Master. If we do not experience that special time of prayer, we will not be broken and burdened over lost souls.

A lady came to me on the first night of a week's meeting asking for my prayers for her husband, who was without Christ. I promised to do so and did pray for him on two occasions with the lady present when I prayed. On Friday evening, her husband came to the service with her. Her face was full of anticipation and hope. I gave an invitation that evening for those who wanted to accept Christ as Savior, and several responded, but not the husband of that lady.

As the people were leaving after the service, she introduced me to her husband and said, "This is the man we have been praying for. I have tried for years to win him to Christ."

His response was quick and very sharp. He said, "I don't understand what you are talking about. There is no difference between your life and my life. We go to the same places, eat the same food, share the same friends, attend the same parties, and watch the same movies and programs; we do everything alike. I can see no difference between the way I live and the way you live."

God help her, he is right. What makes a difference in our lives and the lives of others who do not know Christ Jesus is the amount of time we spend in His presence in fellowship and prayer. You can study the Scriptures and even graduate from the finest Christian schools in the land and know more about the

Lord than anyone in your church and/or community and still not know Him. Knowing about Him is not knowing Him.

Most people who say they do not have the time to meet in secret with God are, in reality, saying they will not take the time to do so. We take time for lunch and breaks twice a day at the job; should we do any less for meeting with God in prayer? God is not seen, nor is He heard, and yet He is there; He is there in secret. Having a meaningful prayer life requires a self-discipline that brings us to a certain place, at a certain time, to meet with our Heavenly Father. Keeping that appointment or failing to keep the appointment reveals how much priority we place on our relationship with God and how much faith we have in Him. It also reveals just how much we love the Father and shows just how slack we have been in the past.

No one who really knows God and falls in love with Jesus and spends special time with Him in fellowship, communion, and prayer will ever leave His presence, nor will they ever grow tired of being with Him in seasons of prayer. We learn to look forward to those times so much that oftentimes we will show up earlier than planned and stay longer than we intended to. It beats the coffee break, lunch hour, dinner, the evening paper, all TV programs, and everything else that has kept us away from Him in the past. We need to think about the time we spend in prayer and determine if it is an inadequate amount of time. If our prayer time is too short, we need to find out why. Start at the top of the list. If He isn't first, make the decision to give Him first place in your life. Life is nothing more than time. When you give one hour to something or to someone, you are giving one hour of your life. Allow the Lord to have the most honored place in your heart, and give it to Him again each and every day. The results will astound you.

As you pray, learn to pray for others, for our country, for international problems, the church, and any other situation you may be aware of. My mother used to tell me she spent the first part of every day praying for her children and the last thing every night before going to bed praying for each one of us by name. I have often heard Mom weeping late at night and in the early hours of the morning. Her love for us was so strong she was driven to the Lord in intercession. How I wish every parent had that kind of compassion and care for their children.

In Matthew 6:7-8, Jesus gave us three instructions about praying. We need to look at them and consider what He is saying to us today: (1) Use not vain repetitions. (2) They thought they would be heard for much speaking. (3) God knows your need. The length of our prayer does not reveal anything of value. The desire of your heart at the moment does, but you cannot persuade the Lord of anything by long prayers. Have you ever become bored when listening to someone pray publicly? If we remember that God knows the need that brought us to Him before we come to Him in prayer, it may well be that God allowed the need to arise just to bring us to Him. When we truly know God on a personal basis, His heart enters into the picture when we pray. We know what He wants from us, and our prayer is an honest and open confession of what is in our hearts. Memorized prayers are said prayers, not prayed prayers. Saying a prayer and praying a prayer is not the same thing.

In counseling over the years, I've come to know people that would come to me on a regular basis with the same problem and say the same words each time they came to my office. It was so disappointing to know they were not really benefiting in any way from my efforts and the time we spent together. I have often wondered if God may not think the same thing. When we come to Him in the same old attitude, say the same things from an empty heart, enter the day and mess up again in the same old way, then go back to God to complain about our weakness and ask for His forgiveness and help, this is evidence of not praying enough.

I have read many books on the subject of prayer and some that set out to teach a person how to pray. There are some helps in these books, but the only way to learn to pray and have an effective prayer life is to pray. You cannot beat on-the-job training when it comes to prayer.

Our time in prayer should be exciting and encouraging. I would suggest at the onset that we not focus on the answers to our prayer but on the fellowship we share with Him. Knowing that we are in His presence and having a dialogue with the God of creation should be enough to excite us. This alone will bring great pleasure to our hearts and strengthen our faith. Of course, God sees and knows what is on our mind, and when He sees the desire of our heart is to experience one-on-one fellowship, He is greatly pleased.

Whatever burdens our hearts is of concern to the Master. We must remember that all that we say before God is of eternal importance. We should never say words to please men or to try to convict men when we are talking to God in public. In private, we must be careful not to include God in the local gossip and/or slander another's name. Prayer is a matter of personal relationship with the Lord and can never be of more value to us than the relationship is. Our prayer life is the visible example of how we value our relationship with Him.

Think about this for a moment. It may prove to be a very sobering thought. Nothing attempted for God can be of greater value than the time and effort spent in prayer discussing the thing we are about to attempt. We cannot measure the value of our prayers by the time we spend in prayer, but we cannot rush through the process of praying, believing all we need to do is mention the need before the Lord. We must learn to express our hearts and allow the Lord to know our thoughts and feelings on the matter we bring before Him. This may take some time, but we must not think we can convince the Lord to answer the prayer just because we labored all night or for hours praying. Again, when we have a relationship with Him, we can know His heart while we pray and learn from experience when it is time to shut up and trust Him.

If God knows our need before we pray, then why pray? We are demonstrating our need for Him, our dependence upon Him. It is a time when nothing else is going on in our mind or heart. We are focused on Him and His love for us. We come to Him as a child would come to a loving father expressing to Him that there is no other and we have no other in mind to trust but Him. We do not need to be so focused on the need we bring to Him that we show disrespect to Him. In fact, if we so focus on Him and His love for us, it may not even be necessary to mention the need. With Him knowing it already and Him seeing our heart bent toward Him in trust, the need will be taken care of. The true value in expressing our needs lies in the fact that He wants to hear us express them. This will become a constant factor in our relationship building with Him.

Bottom line: God ordained prayer as the medium between Himself and us. It is through prayer that His blessings flow into our lives. Each time I receive a blessing from the Master, I instantly question who has been praying for me. Prayer knows no distance and cannot be hindered by national or international disasters. Prayer does not need a visa or permission to enter into a situation where it has been invited.

I want to spend some time in this passage in Matthew 6 on the mechanics of praying. Keep in mind that the goal is to learn how to live above worry and anxiety. I said in the beginning of this effort that there is a parallel between a person's faith and the amount of worry in their life. There is also a parallel between how we pray and the success or lack of success in our spiritual growth.

Jesus was teaching His disciples about prayer in response to their request. They wanted to learn to pray as He prayed. No doubt they had the privilege of hearing the Lord talk to His Father on many occasions and wanted to know the source of His power and His trust in the Father's response. He never demonstrated any doubt about the Father giving what He asked for. He begins by telling the disciples, "After this manner therefore pray ye" (Matthew 6:9). This is an important beginning because He does not want them to repeat His words but to see His efforts to teach them the right approach to prayer and the right manner of prayer. This was to become His example of what a prayer consists of. This was His model prayer; to see His prayer, read John 17. If you study the prayer in John's gospel, note that every aspect of the model prayer in Matthew 6 is utilized.

Jesus knew about God, but He also knew His Father. This is the greatest aspect of prayer taught by the Lord Jesus. He wants us to know about Him, but more so, He wants us to know Him. This can be accomplished in the medium of prayer. Also in this model prayer, we learn that prayer is an act of surrender. We bring all our cares and needs to Him and leave them there in full surrender to His will. Our will is bent or broken by surrender, yielding to His response, whether we get the answer we wanted or something entirely different. If we do not come with surrender in mind, we may be wasting our time pretending to pray, while all we really have in mind is persuading God to do as we want.

Jesus begins His model prayer with the words, "Our Father." "If ye then, being evil, know how to give good gifts unto your children, how much more shall your Father which is in heaven give good things to them that ask him?" (Matthew 7:11). This reveals both our attitude in prayer as well as the Father's attitude. I am a father and love to give good things to my children. I am but mortal; God is divine, and His gifts are far greater than an earthly father could ever give.

We should check out our attitude when we pray to see if there is that fatherly respect and love within us as we approach His throne. The title *Father* requires of us respect and honor, without which we will surely fail to gain our request. Note also the word *our*. This implies at least two things to me: (1) We may not be praying alone. There may be others gathered with us as we pray, and we pray as a unit of believers agreeing as to the need before us.

(2) It implies that we are aware of the needs of others and the suffering of the world around us or confessing the sins of the nation, and we begin by expressing the heavy heart of others as well as our own. It would seem a bit bullish to come into His presence with no need except our own. It reveals a true humble heart when we express brokenness over the needs of others, even before we pray for our own need. I have learned that I can go for many weeks or even months without ever praying for my own needs or desires, spending all my time in prayer for others. On other occasions, I have spent all my time in prayer for myself, only to be reminded that my work is in the interest of others. I cannot appreciate any selfishness about myself and hate it when I become self-centered.

These words, "Our Father," also remind us that we are not the only one praying at that moment and we are not the only one in need. A true heart of compassion allows for the hurts and needs of others. We lift our prayers to the One who sustains the relationship of Father to us, and we are not the only child the Father has. We are members of His family, and there are many children. Prayer should be salted with the dependence we have on our earthly fathers, if we have good fathers. Learn to confide in God. He is approachable and enjoys our coming to Him. We are to see the character of God as firm, compassionate, and loving, as a father should be. This privilege implies relationship, access, protection, education, expectation, and inheritance. It also suggests that we have a duty to trust Him and to pray often. There are also blessings implied in this title, such as love, sustenance, and discipline.

"Our Father which are in heaven." Here is added to the example of how to pray the word *heaven*. The word in the Greek is plural, and there are actually three heavens mentioned in the Scriptures—the air around us where birds fly, the space above where the stars and planets exist, and the region beyond these two, the heaven where God dwells in all of His authority and power. There in that heaven is where our prayers are heard and answered.

Think of all the mighty decisions being made there today. Nations are being changed forever. Climate changes and weather patterns are being altered, decisions about life and death, marriage and family life, and on and on it goes. There at the throne of God, our prayers are heard and forever held in storage. There is the residence of God, the seat of His government, the region of holiness, the abode of angels and saints. There is where He is arranging all the affairs of the universe, receiving the homage of the celestial inhabitants, issuing His commands and executing his threats, attending to the supplication of His people, and protecting His church. There is where our prayers are received.

The point I find in all of this is the influence it should have on all of us as believers. It suggests to me the need to be humble. That I could have a voice in such a place and be heard by such a host of heavenly personalities is very humbling to me. I do not feel worthy of such a privilege. There is a line from a song that says, "But He made me worthy…" I know the measure of His grace, but I still do not feel worthy of such an honor. Thank You, Lord!

This privilege should cause us to be so reverent before Him that we would gladly submit to any and all requirements from Him. In this environment, our spiritual desires should rise far above selfishness and self-centeredness. How could we think of worldly matters while in the presence of our King?

At the same time, there is the air of confidence that comes from the fact that He has invited us to meet Him there, confidence in His love and mercy, not our rights, but the gifts of His love. We must come with the attitude of expectation. How can we say we believe in prayer and not expect the answer to the request we are making of Him? The measure of our faith will be met with the measure of our expectation. I am sure God enjoys seeing us come with the intention of leaving with His answer in hand. To that thought, let me add, don't be afraid to come with big requests. I fear we may disappoint Him when we try to reduce our request because of feelings of unworthiness. It is like putting a price on our prayers. We need to be honest with our request but not be afraid to trust God for big things and big requests, for He is a big God. Could it possible be that the size of our prayers reflects on the way we view God? If we view Him as small and weak, don't you think we might insult Him?

Our prayers should bring us great joy. What an awareness of accomplishment should come over us when we pray. The thought of being invited by the King of heaven to enter into His private chamber is almost too great to fathom. To be received by Him who wishes to be treated as our Father is so great an honor. To realize that along with all the great things going on at that moment He wishes to hear from us should tell us we are special to Him. What a joy to be able to pray and pray with expectation.

It is not the sound of the voice that can enter into the ears of the Lord of hosts but the sighs and groaning of the Spirit. No matter the number of words spoken nor the mixture of words and the sounds of weeping with intense desire, it is the content of our heart that the Master hears and responds to. Only when our words and our heart agree can the voice of the child be heard by the Father. If this were not so, it would be best for all of our churches to begin giving acting lessons instead of Bible study. We would need producers and directors rather than pastors and missionaries. Acting lessons would be of greater value than sermons and prayer meetings. God has chosen what is best for his kingdom, and for His children, He has chosen prayer. It is God's kingdom that should be in focus in the believer when we pray, and our prayer should be in line with His purpose for the kingdom.

Next in the Lord's model prayer, Matthew 6:9, "…hallowed be Thy Name," we are taught how and when the name of God is sanctified.

His name should be sanctified upon us by our righteous deeds and testimony to His divine providence. When we live before the eyes of the public in such a way that honors Him and gives Him praise, the world can see a difference between them and us. This draws attention to the name and purpose of God in our lives.

His name should be sanctified by us in our thoughts, words, and actions. This will be true only when our hearts and lives are in right standing with God—no hypocrisies, no selfish motives, just open and honest submission before the Lord.

His name is sanctified when we are in difficult times. When there is something trying to steal our peace and joy or when dangers come, we can sanctify the Lord's name by displaying the calm and assurance that only a believer can possess. Spend a little time in any hospital emergency department and just observe the reactions to all the different tragic situations brought into the hospital. Many of those people going to pieces are God's children, and the world watching is wondering where the faith and trust in the Lord is. Did God fail them at the moment of greatest need? No? If not, then why are they acting as if they were alone and no one could help or even understand them?

We sanctify the Lord's name when we speak of Him with true reverence. I remember doing a series of messages on the name of God a few years ago. I was so humbled by the power and honor ascribed to His names. I remember reading in Isaiah's prophecy that one of His names is *Wonderful*. Since seeing that, I have not been able to use the word *wonderful* for anything else. If I do slip and say it, I apologize, correct it using another word, and then explain why. Wonderful is one of the names of God, and nothing is wonderful except Him.

We sanctify His name with our actions. Our demeanor reflects what is in our heart. If we are slow to speak and quick to forgive, show respect for all men, and display a meek and gentle spirit, we are honoring His name and causing the world around us to take notice that we are different from the world.

We sanctify His name when we worship. The attitude of our heart, the words on our lips, the tone with which we sing or pray, and the purpose behind all that we say or do tell the world who we are and whose we are. We are to worship together. The Scriptures say, "Where two or three are gathered together in My Name, there am I in their midst" (Matthew 18:20). When we take part in any aspect of worship, we should do so with the attitude of doing it together. When we desire to stand out to be seen or heard above all else, we have missed the idea of public worship.

The seventh and last way we can sanctify His name is in our daily conversation. When we speak with others, we should be holy. Avoid the cheap, sometimes ugly conversations that take place in the workplace or social gatherings. Do not open your ears to the dirty, dishonoring talk of the world. Learn to use words that please the Master, and do not open your mind to receive anything less. Study His name, and learn to speak it with honor and great carefulness, as to never use the name in an unworthy manner.

When God's name is abused in our midst, do not be afraid or ashamed to defend His great name. I heard a man using God's name in vain one day at work. He was telling some kind of story, and in every few words, God's name was being used and abused in profanity. I interrupted the man and asked him what his mother's name was. He told me her name was Martha and asked what that had to do with anything. I explained his use of my God's name is such a way was offensive and told him I did not appreciate it. I suggested that instead of using God's name, he use his mother's name. I was able, some months later, to lead that man to accept Jesus as his Savior. Jesus said in John's gospel, chapter seventeen, that He has given us His name. We should be careful how we use it and how we allow others to use it in our presence. If God's name is not hallowed in our hearts, it will not be hallowed on our lips.

> Wherefore, God also hath highly exalted Him, and given Him a name which is above every name. That the name of Jesus every knee should bow, of things in heaven, and things in earth, and things under the earth. And that every tongue should confess that Jesus Christ is Lord, to the glory of God the Father.
>
> Philippians 2:9-11 (KJV)

There is no other name so highly praised and so worthy of honor as is the name of Jesus. It is not to be used in jokes or crude, vulgar language. I have heard so many respond to such thoughts with the line, "God has a sense of humor." Perhaps He does, but He will never condone disrespect for His name. I, for one, do not believe that taking the Lord's name in vain is limited to just profanity. Any misuse of the name of the Lord is taking His name in vain. One of my professors in seminary used this little analogy; "When God's name is spoken, He turns to see who used it and what the need is. When we speak His name in vain, He has turned to see the need, only to realize His name was used in jest and there was no real need."

As a parent, I learned the tone of my children's voice. It was easy for me to know if there was trouble or pain or seriousness without any words. Only the sound of their voice would tell me their heart. Is that not true with our Heavenly Father? How often has He turned to see the need when one of His children has cried out, "Father"? It is so important that we learn to communicate with Him with words when time allows and when we can find the right words to say. Oftentimes, it seems that I can only come apart from the world and cry, "Father," and nothing more. Yet He understands my need and speaks in reply just as if I had voiced with appropriate words to explain my request.

When we enter our closet place to pray, we must first consider the attitude of our heart concerning our honor of His great Name. So often people will be so focused on their need or request that they have no thought of God at all. Viewed from the human precept, it would appear that the only thing we are interested in is getting what we want. Like a selfish child, all we can say is, "I want," or, "I need," and try to persuade Him how desperate we are and how earnest we are in expressing our need. We must come into His holy presence with Him in mind and in our hearts. We cannot fool God! A selfish child with no real interest in God is not going to receive much, if anything, from the Father.

Have you ever wished God a good day? Do you ever think of all the negatives (humanly speaking) God is exposed to every minute of every day? Begin to think of God in ways of compassion and love. Learn to appreciate all that He does for you and for the rest of the world that is trusting in Him. When I view the affairs of the world, I consider the fact that every power or authority has been permitted by God and is being used to bring about His purpose. Watching the powers of the world move toward the end-times and fulfilling the prophetic scriptures in a perfect manner reminds me that He is in control and has never been out of control. Nothing is happening nor shall anything happen that will take God by surprise or cause Him any delay. His children are all in His care, and His promises are overshadowing us each day. There is no need for us to worry or be anxious about anything because He has everything in His control. What peace, joy, and comfort we should all find in this simple but strong truth.

When we lay all of our cares alongside His provision and care for us, we become so small in comparison it is as if all our cares disappear. It is these kinds of thoughts that should permeate our minds when we come into His presence to pray.

We can move to the next petition in the model prayer: "Thy kingdom come" (verse 10). If we are to envision the greatness of His name and if we are to realize our prayer is rising to the very throne of God, should we not also admit to the authority He will use in responding to our prayer?

The greatest kingdom of the entire world is the kingdom of God. It does not require us to be a professor of history to realize that much of history is the study of failing kingdoms. It is the pursuit of mankind to find a kingdom that will not, indeed cannot, fail. You can see that the kingdoms of the past were built on moral strength and goodness of man. It is for that simple reason the kingdoms of the past have failed. All that man has created or brought into existence is temporal and will fail and pass away. It is the greatness and goodness of God and His work that will not cease to exist and will not pass away.

For now the kingdom of God comes in the brackets of time but one day will come gloriously in eternity. No doubt that one of God's oldest thoughts, if not the oldest thought, is of His kingdom. It has been forever past and continues still today that His kingdom is coming in an inner and personal way to all believers. It is a spiritual kingdom full of morality and goodness.

How far beyond one's selfish interest is the prayer for God's kingdom to come. This is God's command that we pray for the conversion of the world. It is assumed by God that all of His family will be praying for this kingdom to come and reign over men. "Our Father" implies that we all should be concerned to the point of praying that it come to pass. I should think that if we all were intensely praying for such a kingdom, we would be more mindful as to how we live and how we treat our fellow man. I also feel the world would be a different place to live if all of God's people were praying earnestly for His kingdom to come.

There was a time in eternity past that God's kingdom was made up with angels. It was then an undisputed kingdom. If you would see the difference between the kingdom of God and the kingdom of this world, consider the difference in their rulers, their laws, the subjects, the objects, the methods used, and the fact that one kingdom is coming while the other is fading.

This prayer reminds us that there is another kingdom established in the world. It expresses our acquiescence in all things by which the desired result may be secured. It leads us to anticipate that the ascendancy desired will be gained, but slowly, at His pace. With such anticipation, our hearts are always full of hope and will stay full in the future. Take away this hope and all missionary zeal will die or become unfruitful.

We cannot discuss this kingdom without realizing the King of the kingdom. It is the kingdom of Christ and is wholly divine in all its rising and in all of its progress. The scepter of this kingdom is one of invincible strength and dominion. We may be small in number and may want for more power among our members now, but this kingdom is destined to be universal. This kingdom is not yet fully come, thus we must continue to pray, "Thy kingdom come." It should come or already has come to the church.

I am not sure we can say that it is here yet. It needs to first come into our hearts, making us loyal to our King and following all of His directions. How could we earnestly pray for His kingdom to come if in fact we have no such desire in our hearts? If we truly love the Lord Jesus, how could we not respond to His request that we care for and pray for His kingdom? It often appears that we are more interested in promoting the kingdom to which we have pledged our loyalty and the kingdom to which we look for our desires being met. Only when our hearts are full of love for Him and our purpose in life is to enhance His kingdom by our obedience can we truly pray, "Thy kingdom come." There will be no labor on our part in the kingdom and no effort for its advancement until we can express truthfully a love so complete and a yielding to His leadership so satisfying that we can say with all our hearts, "Christ Jesus has first place in my life." This petition is second only to the hallowing of His name and must be seen in its intended order. We can see the intended importance of this petition when we remember the importance of His name.

The third petition in this model prayer is for His will to be done (verse 10). When considering the will of God, we should realize there are three aspects to His will: (1) the secret will of God, (2) the providential will of God, and (3) the revealed will of God, which embraces our sanctification.

Now, if we are to pray that God's will be done, we must gain some insight to what His will is and learn how we cannot only pray for His will but must also do His will. Please note both are required as one. It would be fruitless to pray for God's will if we were not actively seeking to do His will.

In the very beginning of understanding anything about the will of God, we must be aware that this pursuit will require from each of us a special love for God. What is it that will draw complete commitment from an athlete to his/her sport? It is love for the sport. We have seen some very large salaries being paid in some of our professional sports, but even with those monies in the equation, there is still a demand for love. Is it not true with the pursuit of God's kingdom? If we do not love God with all our heart, how will we ever be able to honestly pray for and work in His kingdom?

As members of God's kingdom, let us approach our task daily with a cheerful attitude. I can become so discouraged when I deal with a family or an individual with such a sour attitude about everything and everybody on earth. It is as if they cannot find one good thing to speak about or one reason to praise the Lord. If indeed we are the King's children and have an eternal inheritance reserved in heaven for us, we should be the happiest people on earth. It is not good representation of God's kingdom when we identify with the Lord's people but do so with an attitude of defeat and despair. We should exhibit more joy and more excitement about life than anyone on earth. If our hearts and minds are filled with His goodness, we will be joyful.

It may well be that the problem with the down-in-the-mouth individual lies in their relationship with the Master. Do not fear what the world may think. If you are trusting the Lord and desiring to live for Him, do it with honor and with joy. I am sorry if the world cannot understand my joy. I will not give up my joy, and I will not lose the peace in my heart for any reason the world may give.

In addition to joy, let us respond with great zeal and energy. We may have given the world a false impression by allowing them to believe the children of God are lazy, not dedicated, negative-minded, and uncaring people. If there is anyone on earth that should face the day full of hope, excitement, and a drive to do their best, it is the children of God. There is more possibility before us each day of our life than anyone on the planet.

Whatever we do for the Lord, we should do it with zeal and excitement. Remember who you are and for whom you are working, and allow the spirit of wholehearted commitment surface for all to see. When someone should ask about how you are feeling, find a positive answer to give rather than a negative. Strive to be an upbeat kind of person, showing the happy side of life even when you might be a little down or not feeling so good. Some of God's people want the world to know all about their pains and problems. The truth is, the world cannot do one thing about it, but God can. Keep those things between you and the Lord, and ask Him to improve your situation according to His will and purpose for you.

Make sure your service is offered with humility and reverence. This will help you stay away from all arrogance and pride. Jesus taught us that the last shall be first and the first shall be last. The preferred place in service to the Lord is in the least place. The way God's children get promoted in service to the kingdom is doing all the little things well and with joy. When God sees our faithfulness in the small things, He will promote us to higher positions of service. When God sees us faithful in handling small amounts of money, He will trust us with larger amounts.

Now here is a thought to chew on for a while. When God sees us happy in doing the little jobs because we are doing what He asked and we do our best at it, He can see where our heart is and the desire to please Him, not man, and then promote us in the kingdom. It seems that the norm for today is almost everyone seeking a title or wanting to hold some position of authority in the church. I know of one man who did not meet any biblical requirement for the office of deacon and yet desired the title so much that he quit the church he attended and mussed about the community until he found a small church that would allow him to be a deacon if his family attended. He joined that church, along with his family, but was there only a few weeks until he was asked to resign as a deacon or leave the church.

I see that in the same light of my wanting to pilot the airplane my family is flying on, along with hundreds of other people. I know I cannot fly the plane, and I know that all on board will die, but I want the title of pilot so bad that I actually am willing to try to fly the plane. God help us, we would not get off the ground and would all die in a horrible crash. That man crashed and his family with him, and he did it in the face of all the community.

Why would anyone ever seek a high position in God's kingdom instead of a place to serve where their gift could be applied? What does the title mean if we can't do the job? God has placed us in His kingdom where He wants us to serve. He knows our skills and abilities and knows where He wants us to be. That place of appointment, wherever it is, is the best place on earth to be. It doesn't matter who on earth is watching or what kind of carnal praise is given for that job. It is the Master's "Well done, my good and faithful servant" that gives us the joy of service and the sense of being where we belong. If we are going to pray for His will to be done on earth, we must begin with praying for His will to be done in our lives. If we are not faithful to His calling for us, we are not going to experience His blessings as we should, and we will not grow in faith to the desired place of living above worry.

It is in our perseverance that the world will see us subjected to His authority. It is in our perseverance that He will see us fully given to His kingdom. When we yield ourselves to His leading and commit ourselves to whatever He asks of us and we continue in that service, regardless of what else is going on in the world, He can see, and we can measure our trust in Him.

We tend to want a complete package from Him with full understanding of what may come tomorrow. The truth is, we may never know what tomorrow may bring. We learn to face each day that lies before us without knowing where the next step may take us. Yet because we belong to Him and our faith is focused on Him alone, it does not matter what He may ask of us today. We should and will do our best in order that the world watching will see our devotion, not our skill. They will see our love for our King, not our position of service. In the eyes of God, the doorkeeper at the house of God that does his job to the best of his ability and does it because of his love for the Master will receive the same reward as the pastor in front of the thousands who passed through the doors that the doorkeeper watched. The reward is the same for all the tasks He assigns. If you work at your assigned post for fifty years without complaining and without envy for some other post but in full obedience to the Lord and another works at the same post for six months but with the same zeal and devotions as the first, both will receive the same reward. They both did their best for the Master, and they both did it with all their heart.

God has promised His best for those of His children who give their best for Him. This is what the third petition of the Lord's model prayer is teaching. It is allowing God's will to become the standard and rule of our lives. No need to question His commands, and no need to take extra time to consider and reconsider what He is asking us to do. By simple faith and obedience, we just do it. It doesn't matter what the world may think or say about it; we just do it because we trust the One who asked us to do it. If we respond to His command like this often enough, it will soon become the regulator of our wishes and pleasures. We will find ourselves not wanting for worldly things and not interested in fantasies and winning fortunes on some game show or lottery. This is when God's will becomes our will. It isn't that His will destroys our will, but it's a surrender of our will to His greater and more important will. It is surrendering our love to His love and our wisdom to His wisdom.

The fourth petition in this model prayer is the request for "daily bread." It reflects on the wants of our bodies that are to become subordinate to the purpose of God. This allows us to recognize that our dependence upon God for the supply of our bodily wants is as He wishes it to be.

Through all the years of growing up back in Tennessee, I remember how stern Dad was when we came to the table for a meal. Nothing was allowed until after the blessing was prayed. My father took very seriously the fact that God had provided us with food to eat. Oftentimes we had more than we needed, and Mom and Dad would take all that was left after feeding eight children and themselves to a neighbor they knew would not have enough food. Many times I could hear my father weeping while the children said the blessing. He was so thankful for God's love and blessing us with enough food.

There was not a supply in the house for days to come. Much of the time, we ate what was there for the day and prayed that tomorrow would be the same. One time, Dad brought home a one hundred-pound bag of beans. I felt so rich, knowing that there was food in the house for several days. I did not necessarily like the idea of eating beans three times a day for that period of time, but at least we were eating.

God wants us to ask for and appreciate His giving a sufficiency of supply and not superabundance. This seems to be a major problem today. Almost everyone I talk with is trying to store up an abundance of money for the dark days ahead. I think that sometimes I go too far in the other direction. I have told my wife on several occasions not to buy flour in more than a two-pound bag. I have suggested that I would not want her making bread for another man after I am gone with flour that I had bought. Our hope for tomorrow should not be in the abundance of things we have laid up in store but in God's love and care for us and His promise to provide.

When we grow dependent upon ourselves and our ability to provide all that is needed, our faith grows weak. There is no problem in providing for future days, if we can acknowledge that all we have is supplied by Him. When we know God did the providing, we are careful to use it as He desires, allowing Him to be the Lord of our finances.

Paul wrote something in his letter to the Philippians that has troubled me for some time. In chapter four, verse eleven, he wrote, "Not that I speak in respect of want; for I have learned, in whatsoever state I am, therewith to be content." How could any man say he was content in every matter of life? If he was human and dealt with all the same difficulties that we do, how could he say he was always content?

After years of thought and study, I learned that Paul had surrendered everything in his life to Jesus. He had declared Jesus to be the Lord over every aspect of his living. All that he owned belonged to the Lord Jesus. All the days remaining for him to live belonged to the Lord Jesus.

It can be so with us today. If we make Jesus Lord over our relationship, we will be content with our relationships. If we make Jesus Lord over our employment, we will be content with our employment. If we make Jesus Lord over our income and all our money, we will be content in all our financial matters.

Don't think this is easy to do just because it sounds simple. It will require a death to self and a total surrender to God. It will require us to involve Him in all the decisions of life and make conscious decisions to surrender every area of our life to Him as Lord. We did, after all, take Him as our Lord and Savior. It is easy to want Him as Savior but not so easy to invite Him to be the Lord over all we are and all we do.

Jesus has asked that we not be anxious about tomorrow, what we shall eat, or where we should live. He has promised to provide all that we need if we trust Him. Many today will say they trust the Lord and try to paint a picture of complete trust, but in their heart, there is doubt and hesitation about giving all to Him.

One of the major problems with the matter of abandonment to Christ is the lack of experience. We often want to start trusting the Lord on the larger, more demanding issues of life, and we feel exposed because we have no experience with trusting the Master. I have seen just the opposite also. The believer should not hesitate when trusting Jesus with the smaller issues of life. Nothing is too small or too large for us to bring to Him. What seems to be a big event for you will not seem so large in the Lord's eyes. He does understand our human approach to these issues, having been in the flesh, but He is still God and knows no limits.

The idea is that we learn to trust Him in everyday needs, big and small, and move along with the day, not waiting for Him to respond. Our waiting is often a sign of unbelief or not trusting Him enough to believe it is done when we pray.

"Daily bread" carries two important thoughts with it: (1) God's supply will be daily, if we daily come to Him for the need. (2) *Bread* is indicative of all that is needed for survival. If we take biblical examples of this, we see how strongly the thought plays out.

For example, look at the children of Israel as they leave Egypt. Along the way, the people began to complain about not having bread to eat. So God tells Moses to instruct the people that He would provide the bread they desired but they could only gather enough for one day for each one in the house. If they took more than a daily supply, it would spoil and be worthless. The idea here is enforced; God wanted Israel to come to Him daily for their needs to be provided. This is the same with us today.

Again, let me say God will approve laying by in store as He prospers us, but we cannot lose sight of the fact that He alone is the provider and we need daily intercourse with Him to keep our faith strong and Him satisfied.

If you stay with the story of the Exodus in chapter sixteen, you will remember that Israel then needed meat and fresh water, all of which God supplied in a way that all had to acknowledge it was from the Lord God. Peter wrote in his first epistle, chapter three, verse nine, "God is not slack concerning His promise, as some men count slackness, but is long suffering toward us, not willing that any should perish, but that all might come to repentance." God has not and cannot forget His promise to provide. His terms have not changed from the beginning of time until today. He requires that we believe His Word and trust Him to do all that He has promised.

God is asking us to realize and accept the fact that the source of our supply is in Him. When we try to add to this fact, we weaken His plan and our faith. So many today would have to admit in answer to the question, "What or who is your source of supply?" God and something else. God wants to be our supplier. If He chooses to use some institution or another individual, He will make it known, and all will be taken care of, but we must remember He is the original source.

One thing that gains my attention in the verse is "Give us." This represents the need to be unselfish and at the same time show sympathy for others who are also in need. If we accept the gift from God and know in our heart concern for others as well, we will experience contentment with God's measure of supplies.

I don't know of anything I would consider more selfish than a child of God receiving the supply of God's gifts and then complaining that it was not enough. We are instructed to season our prayers with thanksgiving, showing our gratitude at the time we are presenting our next petition. I must say that as a parent, I am always attentive to the child who is most appreciative for what they receive. When a child expresses an attitude of demand

and no appreciation, I become aware of the need for an attitude adjustment. Our Father gives abundantly and freely and has never failed to meet the need of a trusting child. We should be grateful and express our appreciation for His love by trusting Him even more.

The next petition in the Lord's model prayer is the request for forgiveness of our debts (verse 12). By this prayer, we are reminded of our constant liability to sin. Some people pray, "if I have sinned," while others pray, "since I no longer sin," when the truth is we sin. I hope there is not a pressure to drift in either of the two possible situations.

The Bible teaches that if we say we have no sin, we deceive ourselves and the truth is not in us. We are by nature sinners and subject to failure as long as we are in the flesh. However, that is not a license to sin.

Rightly understood, the real battle with sin begins when we come to Christ. Augustine once said, "The church is not a place where the perfect dwell, but rather a hospital where sick sinners get well." The Christian life is characterized by the struggle with sin. It is this struggle that helps us believe we are indeed born again, for we would not struggle with sin if we were not in Christ Jesus. When we pray for forgiveness, we address the sins of others on the same basis as our own. We tend to see the sins of someone else much greater than our own, but it just isn't so. We are led to separate between the fact of forgiveness and the theory of forgiveness.

Forgiveness can affect our mind, but the value of being forgiven is known in our hearts. The awareness of being clean and without spot before Him is a matter of heart. Forgiveness will always be to us a favor of God and not the result of a claim. I wonder when I hear someone claiming God's promise to forgive their sin if they can ever find forgiveness. God bestows His favor upon us in response to our brokenness and in response to our faith. Wait until you see yourself as being worthy of His forgiveness and you will never come to Christ because you will never be worthy. To claim yourself worthy would imply that Christ should have died on the cross because you are of such value to Him. I have known a lot of good people but never have I found one worthy of the life and death of Christ Jesus.

The petition for forgiveness carries with it the condition for such a request to be granted. "As we forgive those who have trespassed against us" places on us a condition that must be met before we can receive pardon of our sins (verses 14 and 15). In this fifth petition, we acknowledge that before our sin can be dealt with at the mercy seat of God, we must be free of holding a grudge or ill feelings against someone else. We must be able and willing to forgive before we can ask to be forgiven. Think it not strange that this request follows our plea for "daily bread." Can you see the how close the two thoughts are? What is the need for bread if our hearts are full of sin and hatred?

It is so very important for us to learn to come into His presence with clean hearts and motives that are pleasing to Him. If we owe no man forgiveness and we come to the Lord to confess our sins and ask to be forgiven, we shall succeed because it delights the Lord to give such gifts to those ready to receive from His hands.

Sin is seen as a debt to God. It may well be that it is a debt to another someone as well, but it is a debt we owe God, and we cannot be delinquent in paying our debt if we expect to be asking God to forgive us what we owe Him. We tend to set a limit as to how much we are willing to forgive those who sin against us, and yet we expect God to have unlimited forgiveness for our sins. Christ is suggesting to us that we limit God's forgiveness on our sins to the amount of forgiveness and mercy we show those who have sinned against us.

Most of the sins we deal with on earth are petty in size and smaller in importance, and yet they receive the most stern reaction. Most of the sins we commit against God are the worst-case variety, and yet we expect God's full pardon and restoration. How many times will you forgive a brother, until seven times? The Master suggests we should forgive until seventy times seven or on an unlimited basis.

I remember in a very early pastorate trying to get a family that lived very near our church to attend our services. He claimed to be a Christian but would not go to church. After several attempts to persuade him to change his mind, he finally told me his story. He said there was a man in my church that was a liar and a thief, and he did not want to go to church with such men of low character. He continued until he got to the real issue he wanted me to know about. The man he spoke of had failed to pay a $5 debt and later claimed he owed the man nothing. "He told me a lie and then beat me out of my five dollars, and that is stealing. I will not attend church services with such a man as that."

I spoke with the man in our church he had referred to and asked him about the remarks the man had made. The debate over the $5 was questionable at best and childish any way you looked at it. I asked the man for his permission to pay the man the $5 so he could not hold the grudge against him, and he refused. He said that would make it look like the debt was true and that he had not been an honest man. He said he would leave our church so the other man could attend. Neither would agree to meet and resolve the matter, and when I left that community, the two were still at odds with each other. I told them both that I thought $5 was a mighty cheap deal for Satan to use to keep them apart and one of them out of church for so many years.

How foolish we can become when pride gets in our way. What if the man was wrong about his relationship with God and indeed was lost? Would he go to hell for $5? Yet some have gone to hell for less than that. How strong sin can be when all we use to combat it is our own strength and experience. There is only one remedy for sin, and that is to bring it to Jesus in faith, believing He can and will free us from the hold of sin.

As believers, we should always remember that sin in our hearts grieves our Lord Jesus and hinders the work of the Holy Spirit in our lives. Our Father's forgiveness is a sure thing and will not fail. When He forgives, it is immediate and covers all confessed sin when repentance is present. That makes the process complete.

Now allow me to explain this process. It begins with our becoming convicted because of our guilt. The Holy Spirit working in our heart will gain our attention, making us aware that something is wrong in our relationship with God. In John's gospel, chapter eight, verse nine, he writes about people being convicted by their own conscience. The conscience is a major tool used by the Holy Spirit in making us aware of our sin. When the conscience is disturbed, the whole of man can be affected. It may be loss of sleep or constant thoughts that will not subside or anger that seems to take control of our minds. It can push a person to lie or steal and even commit murder, trying to escape a guilty conscience.

However, the conscience cannot be trusted as the sole source of God working in our life to convict us of sin. The conscience can be seared or harden, and we no longer feel the tug of conviction, allowing us to go on in sin without any regret. Everyone does not respond to God's conviction alike, so we cannot always use another person's experience in trying to understand what is happening in our own heart. We must be careful to allow the Holy Spirit free access to all of our heart and all of our thoughts and feelings. We must be honest with Him in describing what we are feeling and thinking. Conviction should lead us to the awareness of contrition.

Contrition is the feeling of sincere remorse for our sin. It is in this state of mind that we become aware of the price of our sin. It may include the damage we have caused to other lives in addition to our own relationship with God. The cause of much contrition is in the realization that we have insulted, offended, and disobeyed the God who loves us so much. Sin in the believer's heart is sin against all that the Lord has done for us, including His death on the cross and all the blessings He has given into our lives. Such sin is remorseful and shameful and should cause us great discomfort and pain.

As the contrition runs its full and deep course, it will lead us to God in prayer, confessing our sins and asking for forgiveness. When this is complete, it will result in the beginning of restoration. We will need to restore our relationship with God and our dependence on Him in faith. We may need to apologize to someone we have offended and ask for human forgiveness. This may prove to be the most difficult thing we do. It is so hard to say those three little words, "I am sorry."

Remember; if we know of acts of sin against another person, we must make every effort to settle things with that person and then come to God to ask His forgiveness. When this has taken place, there will be a sense of burdens lifted, as if a heavy weight has been removed from us. The fear that once held us captive is removed, and the awareness of a fresh sense of freedom returns to our heart and mind. The sleep that had been lost and/or troubled is restored, and our bodies are back to normal. Sin unforgiven carries with it a sense of perplexity because only God can remove it and man is helpless to deal with it alone.

Even if all debt is settled with man, there remains the need to come to God and make our peace with Him. Most sin carries with it the feelings of hatred. Sometimes we may learn to feel hatred toward another person, perhaps someone we used to love. There are times we hate ourselves for being so weak and helpless. Other times, we may cry out in hatred against God as if to blame Him for our failures. Once forgiveness has taken place and all the negatives are gone, the real life of a believer, the child of God, is restored, and we breathe again the fresh air of His love and care.

The next petition in this model prayer Jesus taught, the sixth petition, is, "Lead us not into temptation" (verse 13). God permits us to be tempted for His own glory to discover the freeness and riches of His grace. It is a fact of life; we will be tempted. Temptation, when resisted, will make us stronger in our faith.

Resistance on our part teaches us that we can, by God's help, withstand the things offered to us by Satan. When we win victories over temptation, our Lord wins out over Satan. The church wins out over the world, and the plan and program of God is proven to be the real thing. It is in our resistance to temptation that we cry out to God for strength and oftentimes for His help so that we might stand true to Him and ourselves. In doing so, we have earnestly sought out our place in the body of Christ. We receive our identity and learn about ourselves in relation to Him and to others around us.

There is the tendency to gravitate toward others who are experiencing the same things we are. We must choose our friends and associates well and very carefully. We all need the added strength and comfort of like-minded believers, but we also need a certain amount of exposure to the unbelieving world as well. It is in dealing with these that we sharpen our skills and strengthen our faith. We do not need to avoid the throne of grace; we need to spend as much time there as possible. We profit much from the fellowship with the Master, and we can obtain our assignments as well.

Many believers I know today are accepting their assignments from other people. That is, they learn about needs from people around and respond as if this is what the Lord wants them to do that day. That may prove to be okay and God may indeed use you in that way, but there is a better way. When we have invested an appropriate amount of time in His presence and our willingness to serve is before Him, He will make assignments for us and empower us to accomplish that assignment.

I got to know a real sheep herder in Romania. I learned much about the shepherd and his sheep. I asked the question, "What do you do when some of the sheep begin to stray away from the fold?"

His response was so quick and concise. He said, "I sic the dogs on them to bring them back."

God keeps a close watch over His sheep. When one of us begins to stray, He will ask the Holy Spirit to assign one of us to bring them back.

Serving the Lord has many rewards, both in this life and the life to come. One of my favorites is the joy of doing something with Him. I don't necessarily believe He has to use me, but He allows me to work with Him in bringing sheep to the fold. And I love it. Living among other believers, I feel the Lord uses each of us to strengthen each other and help each one avoid yielding to temptation.

Another role that temptation plays in our lives is to humble us. It would be easy for some to speak about things that they have endured or speak about never facing strong temptation at all. Outward afflictions can and will humble us, but not as temptations do. When we face the reality of being tempted and failing under the temptation, we go to Him for forgiveness and restoration; it is a humiliating experience.

I can remember disobeying my earthly father and getting caught in my disobedience. How embarrassed I was and ashamed to look in his face and see his disappointment in me. It is a thousand times worse when we have sinned and been caught redhanded and must appear before Him and plead for mercy and forgiveness. Is there anything more humbling for the believer than this? I have learned from my own sin and shame that God allows us to experience this in order to conform us to Christ.

Do not forget that Christ was also tempted in all points such as we are tempted. He understands our heart and our mind when we are facing the moment of trial and temptation. Remember, please; He did not sin. He did not give into the temptation, and He has promised us a way to escape every temptation. We must look for the way He has provided and trust Him that it will work, and we shall be delivered.

When we yield to temptation and commit sin and bring our shame before the Lord with broken hearts and wounded pride, pleading for His forgiveness, the hurt of the moment is good for us and must be remembered. When we hurt, we tend to remember a bit clearer. How many times did you touch the top of a hot stove before the experienced pain taught you not to touch the stove again? How many stomachaches did you experience before you learned to watch what you eat and learn that some things you never want to eat again? God would not want us to go through the process of forgiveness and restoration without learning certain lessons that will help us avoid making the same mistakes again.

It will also help us better understand the human race. Your experience with sin and forgiveness is not different than for any other person who has yielded to sin and had their conscience bruised and their faith shaken and been made to see themselves as having failed in their commitment to Him. Remember when Jesus was confronted by the crowd of people who brought to him a woman taken in adultery? The people were demanding that she be stoned and that Jesus should agree with their application of the law. Jesus, seeing the truth about the lady and the truth about those who were accusing her, said, "Let him that is without sin among you cast the first stone." The simple truth was, and is, there were none there that day without sin, so they could not cast a stone. If the Lord requires us to be sinless in order to cast stones at our fellow believers, we will never be able to cast one stone because we are sinners. Again, the failings of others are not so bad when we face our own faults and failures.

Allow me to point to just a few simple rules about dealing with temptation before we move on to the next point: (1) We should avoid all temptation. Do not go toward it, but turn away and avoid it. (2) Learn to resist temptation in the same way Christ Himself resisted. (3) Play close attention to any weak place in your life. Prepare a plan of defense for these weak spots, and pray often for Christ's help and strength. (4) When you stumble, learn to turn these stumbling places into learning experiences. Build on them, and make them into your strong places so you can use them to help others. (5) Learn to never bring others into your temptations. It is part of the carnal nature to want to make accomplices to our failures, believing that somehow that will lessen the hurt of our sin. One of the greatest causes for believers' worrying is the worry about failing to do what we know we should do as Christians. Having accepted His presence with us and in us at all times, we must remember that we are dragging Him along with us when we sin. Every ugly word spoken, every dirty thought passing through our mind, and all the acts of sin committed in the flesh are all in the presence of our Lord Jesus. How the Holy Spirit must feel while we are exposing Him to all of negative things of the world. Instead of sharing in His love and strength, we ask Him to share in our weakness and failures.

The next part of the Lord's model prayer begins the doxology to the prayer. In verse thirteen, we have the thought, "For thine is the kingdom." God's kingdom is universal, over all men and over all things. It belongs to the Lord. It is His eternal right to own the kingdom. He alone can set the standard and the required steps for belonging to His kingdom. It really doesn't matter if you agree or disagree; it is His kingdom, and He is making the rules. If you refuse to abide by His rules, it does not mean you are strong and should be considered by a different set of rules. It only means you are allowing your carnal nature to prove you foolish.

Our accepting the Lord Jesus as Savior and Lord of our life is not just an escapement from hell. It is the choice of a different life, a better life. It is submitting ourselves to a standard of life that is far, far above all other lifestyles. It is not like becoming a member of a club, isolating us from others who choose not to join our club.

When we see and believe in the kingdom of God and pledge ourselves to be a part of His family by faith, we strive to enlist others by making them aware of the benefits of trusting Jesus and living by a standard that can only be achieved by the indwelling of His Holy Spirit. If there were no eternal benefits to belonging to the kingdom of God, the benefits of knowing Him now as our Lord and our best friend and enjoying the daily peace and purpose for life would make it well worth the commitment.

At the top of the list of items we enjoy as belonging to His kingdom is the removal of all wrath. To know God as a friend and no longer a stranger or an enemy is one of the greatest things on earth. It seems as if you cannot go anywhere or do anything without knowing somebody that can pull strings for you. Someone said it is no longer what you know but whom you know that gets you through this world. Well, allow me to add to that thought; there is no person on earth that can equal God when it comes to knowing someone. In fact, you better watch out when you are playing the world's game of pulling strings. If you should use the world's system against one of God's kingdom members, you will be in a lot of trouble. God does not take lightly His children being misused or abused. He cares for His own.

A young lady came to me after a midweek Bible study and prayer service to share with me the abuse she was receiving at her place of work. Her boss had been making some unwanted passes at her, suggesting she must receive them in favor or she could lose her job. The lady had been married only a few years and was raising a one-year-old daughter and needed her job.

In distress, she exclaimed to me, "I don't know what to do." I suggested that we pray about the matter together, and I asked God to defend this lady's rights and to protect her from the unwanted advances of this man. I felt it was just that we file suit in heaven for help and ask our Heavenly Father to oversee the matter.

The next morning, shortly after eight thirty, I received a call from this lady, telling me that when she arrived at her office, the boss was gone. He had been transferred overnight to a different office several hundred miles away. She was so excited to learn that her Father in heaven cared so much for her and her family. Less than six months later, she was promoted to the assistant manager position in that department of a great company. When you mess with the children of God's kingdom, you are messing with God. You should be extremely careful.

In the same way the kingdom belongs to God, so does the power of the kingdom. All the power of heaven belongs to the King of the kingdom, so much power that God can give all that we could ever ask for and more. Now don't begin thinking that all you do is make a wish and God grants it. It isn't that way at all. When we ask God to hear us when we pray, we must come with faith, believing.

The main point I am wanting to make is that we learn to embrace and use the ascending kind of faith that tells us God is with us always, and He knows our needs and is willing to meet those needs when we ask, believing in faith. It isn't a matter of believing that He can meet our needs but that He will meet those needs because of our faith and His promise.

When we limit God by standards, we cut Him down to a mighty small piece of what He really is. I don't even know if the human mind can comprehend God if it comes down to size or power. He is bigger than all the universe and is all powerful. He either causes or permits all expressions of power. When we come to Him with His power in mind, we will begin to ask for bigger answers from God.

God's power is given to us freely, and no one has been excluded from His offer. The power upon the intellectual world is His and has been given to the great minds who, in addition to possessing great mental advantage, can believe with the same faith as the least-educated man. Every person that comes to God for salvation must humble himself in His presence. No matter how great a station he holds in life or how high in society he may be, in God's presence he must humble himself and trust in the same manner as does every other believer. There is only one way in to the family of God, and that is by faith. Having great minds does not give them any advantage over any other believer. It may prove true that with their power of reasoning they can understand certain truths in history and see deeper into the forming of societies that have lived and died since Christ walked on earth, but when it comes to experiencing His love and forgiveness, there is no difference between the two of us.

Walk through the political world, and the same rule remains in place. I, for one, believe the political powers of the world are permitted by God and are in place to serve His purpose. I know it is very rare to find action in the life of a politician that would remind us of God's leading, but He still claims that all in power are according to His purpose. I, like so many, have complained about someone being elected to office against my vote, only to realize later that God must have ordained it because the results of that person being in office advanced the return of Christ and brings the day of our home going even closer. Listen to what God says in His Word. "Let every soul be subject unto the higher powers. For there is no power but of God; the powers that be are ordained of God. Whosoever, therefore, resist the power, resisteth the ordinance of God; and they that resist shall receive to themselves a judgment" (Romans 13:1-2). We do not have to like it, but we are expected to obey the powers to be and do it in a humble fashion so that the people of God do not look like warmongers.

These same truths apply as well to the ecclesiastical world. Within every denomination, there are leaders placed there by God's appointment. It may be that we have had a negative experience in the past with one of these leaders, but we must nonetheless consider ourselves under their authority. It does not change our theology in any way, and we are not puppets doing as they do. The idea is for us to learn to be submissive, without compromise, and display an attitude of peace and love, which is Christ-like.

The duration of this doxology in the Lord's model prayer is "forever." That is a very long time, so we must get it right and get our hearts right in light of the process of prayer. As long as time remains, this requirement is upon us. A lesson so heavy in power, so heavy in duration, and so heavy in importance must be considered with the most grave concern and effort. We cannot afford to miss any part of the teaching and forsake our relationship with Him; we must have confidence in knowing we are doing it right in His sight. He desires us to accept his teaching on prayer and wants us to enjoy the experience as much as He does. The admonition of Paul for us to "pray without ceasing" implies the joy experienced by both the one praying and the One hearing our prayers. Surely when we learn how to pray as He has taught us to pray and to experience the results we receive when we pray, we too, like Paul, will have a prayer in our heart and on our mind and lips all day, every day. We will learn to enjoy the infiltration of the divine and see how advantageous it is to have Him in our life and on our side.

The rest of the world has to depend on worldly systems and worldly response to anything and everything they do. We, on the other hand, as believers, depend on God's love so visible and so real; we embrace His promises and accept His provision for all we need and His direction for where we go. Living among the divine is far better than tolerating a wicked world. Our certainty of success is based on faith alone, plus nothing. There is no limit placed on any of us, except our ability to trust Him. With God, all things are possible. As a man believes in his heart, so it is. It is not faith in our faith but faith in God that gains His attention.

The object of every prayer must be God, and the object of every person's faith must be God. Caution yourself; if you waver, it is because you have taken your eyes off Him and begun to look upon yourself and/or others. We will learn to confirm our prayers as being in God's will, and we will learn to ratify our prayers by ourselves, not by asking others for their opinion. God speaking to each of us will allow us to know we are praying in His will and in His name. No matter what the answer is, we will know that God gave the answer and we can live with it.

We should learn to include praise and thanksgiving in every prayer we pray. Even when we shorten our prayer time for human reasons, there should still be time for praise and thanksgiving. Be careful not to insert words of praise that did not come from the heart, and don't try to convince God of some untruth. He can see the end before the beginning, and He knows all our thoughts and the intent of our heart. If when we go to our place of prayer we have a motive in mind and try to make it as correct as possible, God will know before we call on Him that our motive is not according to His will and purpose. That prayer will not be answered, and God knows it before we say one word. We too should know, before we begin to pray, whether our prayer will be answered or not.

We can know the heart of the Father by faith. When our heart and mind are surrendered to Him, when we know by faith that we are in His presence, when we know the desire of our heart has been placed there by God and prayer is just the process ordained by Him to bring the request before His throne, then our hearts are as one with Him, and then our soul is in communion with God. It is in this situation that we can voice our request in a way that is pleasing to our God; it is then that our language is the very process of praise, for every word spoken is the sound of praise to His ears. It is those moments of acceptance and assurance that we realize He has favored us with the answer to our petition.

It may well prove to be that the experience of praying is greater than the experience of receiving our request. Know they run close together and may be conceived as one in the same; nevertheless, we learn the joy of doing things in His will, His way, and in His good time. The joy of sharing such an experience with Him can easily grow to be far better than gaining His blessings. What greater blessing could the soul receive than the awareness of being as one with Him? Here we can see that praise (real praise), not man-made pretense, is faith in action and the anticipation of heaven. That environment is what we can expect in heaven and forever. It is the greatest bond of union that man can experience. It is God's special gift to all who trust Him and wait in faith, believing they shall receive the fullness of His glory and the richness of His blessings.

Summary

The apostle Paul, writing to Timothy the second time, in chapter three and verse one, said, "This know, also, that in the last day perilous times shall come." Then he goes on to write about many of the coming events and descriptions of people living during that time. It is my belief that we are now in those days just before the return of our Lord Jesus to earth to take His children home. The perilous times are a mixture of social ills that have plagued the world, deceived many people, and left behind a trail of worry and anxiety. We would be hard pressed in any business in the world today to find more than a few people that are not worried beyond any sense of reason. The economy is failing in most nations, and here at home in America we face great financial difficulties. Add to this the great number dealing with illegal drugs and various addictions, and it would be easy to assume that most of the world is struggling to deal with serious levels of worry and anxiety.

It is as if most of the people we talk with each day are being treated for stress and/or depression. It is not just the normal routine of worry. There are many today that are so acclimated to worry, excessive worry, and depression that it is the normal way for them to feel. They are living with a physical danger, but to them, it is the norm. Excessive worry and/or depression can lead to many abnormalities. Some of these have reached into the lives of our children as well. Feelings of emptiness, hopelessness, or worthlessness are seen all too often. I speak with people every day that tell me about feelings of guilt and how they pretend to be preoccupied to avoid being confronted. In every business there are those struggling with loss of interest in activities and pleasurable things, like hobbies. Some have loss of appetite and trouble sleeping; others have trouble remembering and concentrating or making decisions. They are withdrawn from friends and family, and some even speak of having hallucinations. All of these symptoms are serious and need professional help.

It is not so unusual for a spiritual problem to turn into a physical problem. Sometimes when we find ourselves dealing with the negative effects of sin, we can turn to God's comfort and forgiveness and move on with victory and healing. It is possible to have injured our faith to the point that we cannot bring ourselves to trust God or turn to Him for His forgiveness. I am so sure that God wants all who are dealing with stress, worry, or anxiety to come to Him, to trust His Word and receive His promises to replace that worry with hope and restore the calm peace of His presence in that troubled heart.

The world is painting a picture that says to look around at the many people worried and stressed out of measure, but God is inviting us to look to Him and see the hope and healing that only He can give. God has made it possible for all of His children to live a life free from the kind of worry that will destroy the good things of this life. I am persuaded that the only way we can enjoy this gift from God is to learn to trust Him completely and embrace His promises with the ascending faith that requires our Lord to respond to His children's cry.